A Man for All Seasons

Robert Bolt

Revised Curriculum Unit
3rd Edition

Harcourt A. Morgan

Contributors
Helen Jean Novy
Elaine Schindler
Christine West

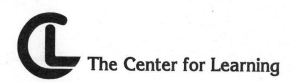
The Center for Learning

The Publishing Team

Rose Schaffer, M.A., President/Chief Executive Officer
Bernadette Vetter, M.A., Vice President
Diane Podnar, M.S., Managing Editor
Amy Richards, M.A., Editorial Director

Cover Design

Clare Parfitt

A Man for All Seasons (3rd Edition) is a revision of
How to Read a Play © 1977 and *Experiencing Drama* © 1983,
both Center for Learning publications.

List of credits found on Acknowledgments
Page beginning on 91.

ISBN 1-56077-118-6

Contents

Introduction

The two-act drama, *A Man for All Seasons* was written by Robert Bolt, one of England's most prolific script writers and playwrights. American students may know him best for his writing of the screen play for *Dr. Zhivago*.

This drama is an ideal vehicle for high school students to ponder the problem of commitment to private conscience as opposed to acceptance and adaptation to corruption for comfortable survival. Although the historical events selected as background for the major theme of the drama are far removed from the democracy taken for granted by most students, the conflict is both timely and universal. The dilemmas that faced the politicians, noblemen, and commoners in the early sixteenth century during King Henry VIII's reign have their moral counterparts in today's world.

Students will be challenged to explore their own values and goals in a time frame in which they are often labeled as materialistic, non-committed, and self-centered. Thomas More's inherent goodness stead-fastly pitted against his realm's equivocation may evoke an awareness that there are issues and causes today for which people of conscience sacrifice their own comfort and safety. They may even empathize with the play's main character who, in 1937, was declared a martyr-saint at the Vatican in Rome. They perhaps will develop a degree of heightened sensitivity toward the ideals of brotherhood, integrity, and justice as they become witnesses to a piece of history in which a virtuous, innocent man was entrapped by lies, self-interest, and ambition devoid of conscience.

A careful study of this powerful drama encourages thoughtful self-analysis, focusing on two important questions:

Am I a *Man for All Seasons* or am I the *Common Man*?

Is Thomas More a hero whose ideals should serve me as a reminder of the human potential for climbing up amongst the stars rather than groveling down in the dust?

Teacher Notes

The lessons in this unit are based on the use of the edition published by Vintage Books, New York, 1962.

The lessons are sequential, each designed for a single class period, but subject to a varied time allotment in accordance with emphasis on student needs.

A basic principle of this unit is that peer group interaction is an important function in the learning process. Sharing and evaluating ideas develops skills in recognizing the logic and validity of conclusions to assigned problems. Small group work also affords teacher-student interaction, thus creating a pleasant and confident learning atmosphere.

Assignments include handouts for the study of historical background, for analysis and discussion of literary form and major ideas of the drama, and for journal notes and writing entries.

In addition to the lessons and handouts, supplementary materials include historical background details, activities for presentation of the play, objective tests, and suggested topics for essay writing.

Available films, slides, pictures, tapes, recordings, and other dramas of related conflict (*St. Joan*—G. B. Shaw; *The Crucible*—A. Miller; *Antigone*—Sophocles) will enhance students' understanding and satisfaction in the study of *A Man for All Seasons*.

Videocassette: *A Man for All Seasons*, 134 minutes, color.
The rivalry between King Henry VIII and Sir Thomas More is chronicled in this Academy Award-winning film starring Paul Scofield, Robert Shaw, Orson Welles, and Vanessa Redgrave. (Zenger Video, 10200 Jefferson Boulevard, P.O. Box 802, Culver City, CA 90232-0802, 1-800-421-4246)

Lesson 1
Historical Background

Objectives

- To review the historical background necessary to understand the play
- To define unfamiliar terms encountered within the text

Notes to the Teacher

Students will enjoy this play more if several stumbling blocks are removed. Because it presents a piece of early sixteenth-century history, the reader-viewer needs preparation for understanding the context from which the drama is drawn. Most of the characters were born into the aristocratic class, practiced in the affairs of state, and schooled in the intellectual trends of the times making their dialogue and references to pivotal events, people, and ideas of their day totally foreign to today's students.

One approach to preparing students for this historical background is to refer to the information given in Bolt's preface to the text which mentioned only basic facts. A more effective method is to assign students research topics to share with the class. These subjects can be issued on a voluntary or required basis depending upon the achievement level of the group. A suggested list of research topics is included. A third approach is to reproduce and present the information on King Henry VIII and Sir Thomas More provided in the Supplementary Materials.

A list of dates which chronicles More's life and significant events in the play is included in **Handout 1**. Students should keep this for reference throughout this unit.

Several terms essential for appreciation of the play are also part of **Handout 1**. Students should be required to learn these terms for use within the context of the drama. The handouts should be kept for reference.

Procedure

1. Issue **Handout 1**. Require students to become familiar with the dates so that they have the necessary historical sequence clearly in mind. Discuss this chronology to fix it firmly in the students' minds. (This handout may also be used as a transparency to facilitate classroom discussion and clarification.)

2. Distribute **Handout 2**. Tell students to write definitions of the terms which can be found in the dictionary. Remaining items will require the use of encyclopedias or other historical reference works. If some students are assigned to present special class reports, inform the class to take notes to complete their sheet.

3. Listed below are possible research topics which students may present to the class. These may be given to individual students or small groups.
   a. Cardinal Wolsey
   b. Thomas Cromwell
   c. Sir Thomas More
   d. Henry the VIII
   e. Martin Luther
   f. Machiavelli; *The Prince*
   g. The Catholic Church and Church of England, 1450–1547
   h. War of the Roses and the Tudors

Important Dates and Events

Directions: You will need to be familiar with these dates and events. They will assist you in keeping the events and characters in the play in proper chronological perspective.

1478—More's birthdate

1491—Henry's birthdate

1496—Richard Rich's birthdate; died in 1567

1502—Henry's brother Arthur died. He had married Catherine of Aragon eighteen months earlier.

1504—More elected to Parliament at age twenty-six.

1509—Henry married Catherine of Aragon and at the same time became king.

1515—Wolsey became chancellor and head of both state and church under Henry.

1517—Placement of Martin Luther's "99 Theses" on Wittenberg Cathedral, starting the Reformation.

1518—More's first year of service to Henry VIII as a member of the King's Council

1521—More helped King Henry write "A Defense of the Seven Sacraments"; Henry named "Defender of the Faith" by the pope.

1527—Henry VIII decided to divorce Catherine of Aragon and attempted to marry Anne Boleyn.

1530—Wolsey died November 29 before being sent to the Tower of London.

1531—Submission of clergy in convocation to Henry's threat of limitation of their powers if they didn't switch allegiance from pope to him

1532—More resigned as chancellor in May after thirty-one months in office.

1533—Henry married Anne Boleyn in June.

1534—In April, More was taken to Tower of London because he would not sign the Act of Supremacy.

1535—On July 7, More was executed.

1540—Cromwell executed in July.

1547—Rich became Chancellor of England until 1557 (resigned due to ill health). King Henry died.

1556—Cranmer burned at the stake in March.

Puzzles Prior to the Play

Directions: Define or explain each of the following. You may find the information in a standard dictionary or in an encyclopedia or other historical reference text.

1. causeway

2. martyr

3. convocation

4. heretic

5. dispensation

6. bracken

7. Machiavelli and his book *The Prince*

8. Socrates

9. Erasmus

10. Tudors and Yorkist Wars (The War of the Roses)

11. Moloch

12. Martin Luther and the Reformation

Lesson 2
People in the Play

Objective

• To clarify character description

Notes to the Teacher

A major problem often encountered in the study of this play is that students cannot keep the characters identified easily. They find the information in the "People in the Play" section of the text difficult to grasp unless given some assistance.

Handout 3 will help resolve this difficulty. Students must thoroughly understand the subtle traits and driving motivations of these characters in order to grasp the intensity of conflict and to relate it to modern times.

Inform students that they are to keep this handout throughout their study of the play to refresh their memories frequently.

Procedure

1. Distribute **Handout 3**. Time will be best utilized if the class is divided into groups of three since most of the major numbered items on the handout have three subtopics.

2. Ask students to describe to the class, either individually or in groups, one of the characters. Require them to use in their description the terms and/or phrases from **Handout 3**. This will insure that the class gets a complete overview of the characters. Instruct students to take careful notes as these descriptions will be invaluable to them in future assignments.

In Search of . . . Character

Directions: Write a definition in your own words for the terms or phrases which are listed for each character. These descriptive terms are taken from the "People in the Play" section which appears just before the play's text begins.

1. The Common Man
    a. Crafty

    b. Loosely benevolent

    c. Base humor

2. Sir Thomas More
    a. Robust

    b. Debonair

    c. Ascetic

3. Richard Rich
    a. Studious, unhappy face

    b. Fire of banked-down appetite

    c. An academic hounded by self-doubt

4. Duke of Norfolk
    a. Rigid adherence to the minimal code of conventional duty

    b. Moral and intellectual insignificance

    c. Untouchably convinced

5. Alice More
    a. Hot-hearted

    b. Defiant

    c. Worships society

6. Margaret More

    a. Ardent moral fineness

    b. Reserved stillness

7. Cardinal Wolsey

    a. Megalomaniac ambition

    b. Lonely den of self-indulgence and contempt

8. Thomas Cromwell

    a. Subtle

    b. Self-conceit

    c. Intellectual bully

9. Signor Chapuys

    a. Lay ecclesiastic

    b. A mental footpath as narrow as a peasant's

10. William Roper

    a. All-consuming rectitude

    b. Solace

11. Thomas Cranmer

    a. Theologian

    b. Lacks deep religious convictions

Lesson 3
Preplay Experiences

Objectives
- To promote a careful reading of and an active involvement with the characters, props, and incidents of the play
- To establish concrete visualization of each character

Notes to the Teacher

In this lesson, the teacher will draw the class into active preparations for entering the play by issuing cards to selected students which identify the characters, appropriate props, and distinguishing traits necessary for the actor to carry out a role. This activity may be developed in several ways. You may wish to have these selected students role play the entire drama as a method of having the class interact with the text. Another approach may be to present some of the more difficult scenes such as the argument between King Henry and Sir Thomas, the breaking of More's friendship with Norfolk, the jail cell discussion, and the final trial. You may desire to clarify the Common Man's roles by having each of those six students relate his role to Bolt's introductory comments about the Common Man. Since there are many characters for students to keep clearly in mind, each actor could be called upon from time to time to remind the class of his or her distinguishing traits or actions.

Procedure
1. Reproduce a sufficient number of cards from **Handout 4**. Make a single copy of the cards numbered 1 through 23. You may wish to make additional cards identifying non-specified roles, such as other logical members of More's household staff or members of the jury, to provide at least a sympathetic stance toward some aspect of the conflict to students without cards.

2. Before cutting apart the cards for **Handout 4**, you may want to duplicate the last page of **Handout 4** on the backs of the copies. This page depicts a coat of arms for the House of Sir Thomas More. It might give the cards an official air and may lead to some activities for a later project in heraldry.

3. These cards may be distributed in the introductory class of this unit, or they may be issued a few days prior to the class study of the play. The cards should be self-explanatory, and students should be encouraged to review the text and prepare for their parts. Be prepared, however, to answer any questions which arise as students may still be somewhat baffled by historical contexts and difficult concepts at this early stage.

Assignment

Read the Common Man's speech which opens act 1.

Cards of Fate and Fortune

. . . .

1

A. You are a peasant woman wearing an apron or a frilled tie bonnet.
B. You will present a silver cup to Sir Thomas just before the first speech of the play.
C. You can make the cup simply by covering a cup with foil.
D. You will have lines in act 2 at which time you will be angry and vengeful at Thomas because he rendered a verdict against you.

. . . .

2

A. You are Thomas More's servant.
B. Your props include a basket with a jug or flagon and five silver cups, one larger than the others.
C. You pour yourself a cup at the opening of the play.
D. You can cover a bottle or pitcher and five cups with foil.
E. Rehearse the opening speech of the play by the Common Man, your character.
F. After delivering your opening speech, follow the stage directions carefully, such as the one telling you to pour a cup of wine, etc.

. . . .

3

A. You are Thomas More, a lawyer and magistrate, friend of King Henry VIII of England.
B. You should take the cup of wine when it is offered to you by your servant, Steward, also known as the Common Man.
C. Try to find a black cloak or an academic gown or a gavel as symbol of your legal and judicial profession.
D. You will give Richard Rich a silver goblet which you will have received earlier.
E. At the following cue you will link hands with your wife, Alice, and your daughter Margaret: "Now you'll go to bed . . ." (act 1). Recite the speech in unison.

. . . .

4

A. You are Richard Rich, a young Englishman aspiring to rise higher with "important" people in England so that you can secure a position of public prestige and financial reward.
B. You are willing to bribe someone to obtain information that you can then use to buy your way into "friendship" with higher officials.
C. You need some coins covered with silver or gold foil and possibly a money pouch out of which to draw them to "pay" Thomas More's servant for some information.
D. Give him the money at the cue line according to the stage directions in your dialogue in act 1.

. . . .

. . . .

5

A. You are the Duke of Norfolk.

B. You like to hunt with falcons specially trained to attack. Bring a symbol of your hunting hobby, either a bow and arrow or quiver. A big leather-looking glove with a real or artificially appended cuff chain hanging from a finger or wrist for securing the hunting bird and a head-helmet for blinding the bird are optional.

. . . .

6

A. You are Alice More, Sir Thomas More's wife.

B. You live very comfortably at the opening of the play while your husband is in the favor of the king. You will eventually be separated from your husband and go to visit him bringing him some of his favorite foods.

C. Fill a basket with contents resembling a hunk of cheese, custard, and a bottle of wine, and, perhaps some rolls or bread.

D. At the following cue, you will give the basket to your daughter Margaret to hand to your husband: "We've brought you some things. Some cheese . . ." (act 2).

E. At the following cue, "Now you'll go to bed . . ." you will link hands with your daughter and husband and recite the speech in unison.

. . . .

7

A. You are Margaret More, daughter of Thomas and Alice More, and quite a scholar having been taught Latin by your father and Greek by a friend. You enjoy hunting by horseback with falcons and are on the verge of being engaged to William Roper.

B. Collect some sticks and long twigs and tie them in a bundle. At the appropriate moment, you will toss the bundle of sticks at your mother's feet.

C. You will remove the chain and medallion, symbol of the second highest office in England, from your father's neck at his request at the sad moment of his resignation in act 2.

D. At the following cue, "Now you'll go to bed . . ." you will link hands with your father and mother and recite the speech in unison.

. . . .

8

A. You are a publican (more commonly known as an innkeeper) who does not want to become involved with the dangerous affairs surrounding More.

B. Bring a serving tray with two beer mugs to balance on it. Wear a bartender's apron.

C. You appear in the last scene of act 1 as you show Rich to the private meeting room where Cromwell is waiting for him.

. . . .

9
A. You are Cardinal Wolsey with the high rank of Lord Chancellor of England when the play opens.

B. Make a red cardinal's hat for yourself. You might also obtain a red cloak to wear around your shoulders as another symbol of your role. But, hang on to your hat; there are those who might advise the king to have you beheaded. Bring a candle because your rendezvous with Sir Thomas More is at night.

C. You are wearing a chain with a medallion which you can make by covering an oval-shaped piece of cardboard, two inches by one-and-one-half inches diameter, with a piece of aluminum foil.

D. After completing your dialogue with More, act 1, hand your hat and cloak to the Common Man.

10
A. You are the boatman.

B. Make or obtain a boatman's or sailor's hat.

C. Make yourself a flashlight lantern for travelling up and down the Thames River at night with important personages who, you feel, underpay you when you have to row against the current.

D. Accept coins from your passengers and deposit them in a drawstring pouch or something similar.

11
A. You are Signor Chapuys, the Spanish ambassador.

B. You are seeking information for your king and your country. You are willing to bribe Sir Thomas More's servant to find out information about More's learnings in regard to Henry VIII's desire to divorce his present wife, the Spanish Princess Catherine, who had been the wife of Henry's brother, now deceased. The marriage to a deceased brother's wife had required a dispensation from a practice on the discipline level of Church Law. The pope had granted the dispensation. You represent the King of Spain who is Catherine's nephew. You both want Henry to keep her as Queen of England.

C. You need some coins covered with silver or gold foil and possibly a money pouch out of which to draw them with which you will "pay" Thomas More's servant for some information.

D. Give him the money at the cue line according to the stage directions in your dialogue in act I.

12
A. You are William Roper, a friend of the More family, who is in love with Thomas More's daughter, Margaret.

B. Bring in something resembling a decanter of wine (bottle).

C. You will present this bottle of wine to Sir Thomas More when you and Margaret and More's wife Alice visit him in jail (act 2).

A. You are the King of England, Henry VIII. You will confer a chain and medallion, symbol of the highest office in England after the king, "on" or "to" Lord Chancellor of England. You will place the chain around the neck of Sir Thomas More, a magistrate friend of yours.

13 B. Make a medallion out of cardboard and foil.

C. Confer the medallion at these cue lines: "England's next Lord Chancellor was Sir Thomas More . . ." (act 1).

D. You might want to look up something about Henry VIII in an encyclopedia: you might also want to check the definitions of "magistrate" and "chancellor."

A. You are a jailer in the Tower of London.

14 B. Bring a big key ring with a lot of keys or make large skeleton keys out of cardboard (covered with foil and hang them by a string from your belt.

C. Admit Sir Thomas More to "jail" at the end of the cue line: More: " . . . Our natural business lies in escape—so let's go home and study this Bill" (act 2).

A. You are Thomas Cromwell, advisor to King Henry VIII.

15 B. You are seeking information for the king and are willing to bribe someone for it. Your duty is to get the church and Sir Thomas to approve of the marriage of Anne Boleyn.

C. You need some coins covered with silver or gold foil and possibly a money pouch out of which to draw them to "pay" Thomas More's servant for some information.

D. Give him the money at the cue line according to the stage directions in your dialogue in act 1.

A. You are a diplomat, attendant to the Spanish ambassador to Signor Chapuys.

16 B. Bring a cloak or a coat or a scarf to drape over your master, the Spanish ambassador.

C. As a "stooge," plan to stand in the background flanking Signor Chapuys from the following cue line, at which time you place the cloak over his shoulders: Chapuys: "For sheer barbarity, commend me to a good-hearted English woman of a certain class . . ." You: "It's very cold, Excellency" (act 2).

A. You are Thomas Cranmer, Archbishop of Canterbury. It is your duty to persuade Sir Thomas to agree to Henry's marriage to Anne Boleyn and the split with the Catholic Church.

17 B. Be patient, because you are the last of the named characters to appear in the play and do not have lines or actions until the second to the last scene, the trial.

C. Bring a Bible for the solemn swearing in of Richard Rich officially called forth by Cromwell to testify.

D. Offer the Bible to Richard Rich who will place his left hand on it and repeat after you: "I do solemnly swear . . ."

A. You are in service in Thomas More's household.

18 B. Rest comfortably and with pride in your master's service until Sir Thomas refuses to speak his mind about the Act of Supremacy.

C. You can wring your hands and long for the good old days as the play draws to a close and you are put out of work.

A. You are one of the common rabble swayed easily to the purposes of the king whom you idolize.

19 B. Gape at the king and the machinations of the ministers of his court. Be glad that you are not involved.

A. You are a member of the nobility striving to maintain inherited powers, special privileges, and the favor of the king.

20 B. Be cunning in your observations, deferential to those the king has empowered, and shunning to those in disfavor with the throne.

C. Hold on to your head!

A. You are a member of the clergy.

21 B. As an ordained Churchman, maintain your power and privileges by going along with whatever the king desires.

C. Rubberstamp the king's Act of Supremacy and smooth over ecclesiastical difficulties in accepting it. Do not allow yourself any examination of conscience.

A. You are the jury foreman. It is your duty to announce to the court the verdict upon which the jury decides.

22 B. You will need to wear a juryman's hat which may be a traditional modern executive's hat.

C. You strike an attentive pose during the trial. When Cromwell calls for an immediate verdict, you are willing to give him the one he wants because you are fearful of the repercussions of making him angry.

A. You are the traditional headsman. It is your professional duty to carry out the sentence of the court—the beheading of Sir Thomas.

23 B. Wear the customary black hood and bring a replica of an ax.

C. You will have only one line at the play's conclusion, but some role playing will be required.

"Perhaps we *must* stand fast a little—even at the risk of being heroes."

"Perhaps we *must* stand fast a little—even at the risk of being heroes."

"Perhaps we *must* stand fast a little—even at the risk of being heroes."

"Perhaps we *must* stand fast a little—even at the risk of being heroes."

Lesson 4
Reading for Comprehension

Objectives
- To develop a broader understanding of important ideas in the play as embodied in one major character
- To develop an understanding of complex uses of language found in the play

Notes to the Teacher

This lesson is planned to assist students in tackling the greater complexities of language and philosophy which they will encounter in this drama. Students will come to understand the entire play more clearly if they first know one character thoroughly. This objective will be met by the compilation of a journal which will consist of activities accomplished and information gathered throughout study of the text. The first four handouts of this lesson comprise the ongoing journal project for students while they study the play. The fifth handout is meant to guide them into a careful textual reading.

When finally submitted by the student at the end of this study, the journal will first include **Handout 5** which gives instructions for gathering the main body of information from five or six scenes of the play about a character of their choosing. Students will record this on their own paper. **Handout 6** is a creative exercise in heraldry which will end their views of the character. **Handouts 7** and **8** will form three appendices to the journal. They ask students to deepen their understanding of the text by explaining vital quotes, discussing philosophy, and writing two epitaphs.

Handout 9 requires students to read the Common Man's first speech and the opening of the first scene carefully, so that they are aware of the important ideas. It will also signal that this is a piece of literature that must be read with care and understanding.

Procedure
1. After students have a familiarity with the characters distribute **Handout 5** as an assignment due when they have completed their study of the play.

2. Students will choose a character whose point of view they can understand. (It is best that they not choose Sir Thomas More, as he will be the basis of most class discussions. This will force students to read more carefully about the other characters.)

The "scenes" indicated in the left column of the handout are arbitrary divisions as Bolt's play has only two acts with no scenes indicated.

3. Issue **Handout 6**. Remind students that they already have a facsimile of Sir Thomas More's coat of arms on their cards of "Fate and Fortune." Tell them to use their imagination in creating this emblem but to base it on specific clues from the text. Tell them to be able to provide those clues for the class. Encourage them to refer to the "Heraldry" section of an encyclopedia for guidance concerning historical background, types of coats of arms, and the colors, shapes, and emblems used to design them.

4. Distribute **Handout 7** and **Handout 8**. Explain to students that this material will be attached at the end of the journal. The "Quotable Quotes," "Statement of Philosophy," and "Epitaphs" will be developed for their chosen character only.

5. Ask students to follow their texts as you read carefully through the Common Man's opening speech. Then issue **Handout 9**. Ask students to work independently in choosing their answers. Inform them that they will need to refer to dictionaries, work carefully from the context of the speech, and make some good guesses. In some cases, there may be more than one acceptable answer, but they will have to be prepared to support their choices. Suggested Responses:

1. a	6. c	11. d
2. d	7. b	12. b
3. e	8. b	13. a
4. b	9. b	14. a
5. b	10. d	15. b

6. After students have worked individually on the handout, let them help each other. When most have completed the answers, discuss their responses as a class and try to reach a consensus of understanding.

Assignment

Read scenes 1 and 2 of act 1 (through Wolsey's conversation with Sir Thomas).

A Chronicle of the Times

by _____

Directions: This will be a journal which you will write as though you were one of the people in this historical drama. Choose a character other than Sir Thomas More. Summarize and react to the events of the play from that character's point of view. From the Major "Scenes" section in the left-hand column below, select five to six "scenes" as the bases of your entries. Use the questions given in the right-hand column as a guide for your character's responses. Your journal entries must be made on your own paper of this same size (8½" x 11").

Major "Scenes"	Questions to Be Answered for Writing the Chronicle Journal
Act 1	**Character I am:** _____
1. More's Chelsea home	Questions I am answering:
2. Middle of the night with Wolsey at Richmond	1. What happened? (Who talked to whom? Why?)
3. Dockside with Cromwell, Chapuys, etc. at Richmond before dawn	2. What I felt about it
4. Morning back at Chelsea	3. What I think I should do
5. Hampton Court (bribery scene)	4. What I wish others would do
6. Cromwell and Rich at the pub	5. What I feel will happen next
	6. Why it is important to the ideas of the play

Act 2	Scenes I'm listing for my entries (In order of appearance)
1. Announcement of the Act at Chelsea	1. _____
2. Cromwell's office at Hampton Court	_____
3. Sir Thomas More's home at Chelsea	2. _____
4. Cromwell's office at Hampton Court	_____
5. The riverside at Hampton Court	3. _____
6. Tower of London	_____
7. Tower of London	4. _____
8. Trial at the Hall of Westminster	5. _____
9. Death scene at Tower Hill	6. _____

Coat of Arms

Directions: Create insignias to identify the character whom you have chosen to chronicle the plot of *A Man for All Seasons*. Follow the directions given on the reverse side of this sheet. You may want to refer to the "Heraldry" section of an encyclopedia for guidance in the preparation of your character's family emblem.

Coat of Arms

A Coat of Arms designed for _____

Coat of arms designed by _____

1. Divide the shield (escutcheon) into sections, for example, use bars, diagonals, or a cross.

2. Adopt emblems for your character, such as:
    a. animals—deer, lions, horses, birds, rabbits
    b. man-made objects—castles, swords, keys, shovels, pens
    c. nature—trees, flowers, fruit

3. Choose a metal and a color ("colors") for your coat of arms and color it in.

    or—gold or yellow   vert—green
    argent—silver or white   sable—black
    gules—red   purpure—purple
    azure—blue

4. Write a motto for the character and print it on the scroll.

5. Explain the significance of the various elements of the coat of arms you have designed for you character. Write these comments below.

Divisions

Emblems

Colors

Motto

Appendix 1

Quotable Quotes

Directions: This will be the first appendix to your journal. Give at least three important quotes spoken by your character. First, identify the scene from which it is taken; then, write the quote; next, briefly explain why it is important in understanding your character.

1. Scene

   Quote

   Importance

2. Scene

   Quote

   Importance

3. Scene

   Quote

   Importance

A Man for All Seasons
Lesson 4
Handout 8 (page 1)

Name_____
Date_____

Appendix 2

Philosophy

Directions: In the space below, discuss what you see as being the philosophy of your character. First, however, explain the phrase "philosophy of life" as you understand it after studying Lesson 9.

Definition

Philosophy of your character

Appendix 3

Epitaphs

Directions: Epitaphs are usually engraved on tombstones. They are sayings that were either favorites of the deceased person or which were characteristically appropriate for him or her. Select two epitaphs which you think would effectively suit your character and write one in each of the markers below.

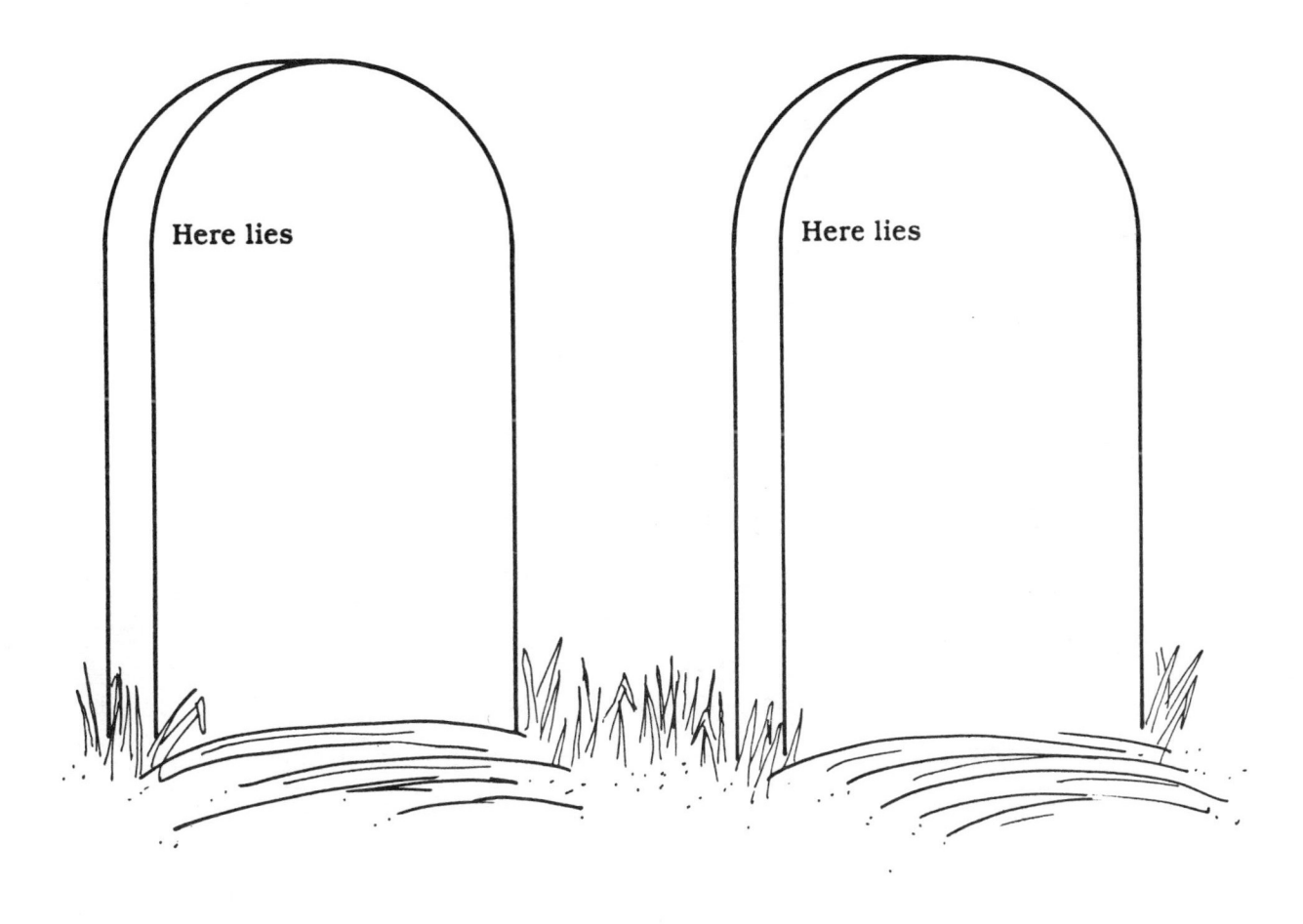

The Common Man's Uncommon Speech

Directions: Write the letter of the best answer on the lines provided.

_____ 1. When the Common Man as narrator at the play's opening uses the phrase "majestic meanings," he means
   a. pretended important statements
   b. big, incomprehensible words
   c. the king's pronouncements

_____ 2. When he refers to "closely woven liturgical stuff," he means
   a. Church vestments
   b. fine linen garments
   c. appeals to Church pronouncements
   d. references to formal religious statements
   e. apparel for attendants in the House of Lords

_____ 3. When he says that others speak with "embroidered mouths," he means that
   a. they use a lot of lipstick
   b. they are tight-lipped and silent
   c. their lips are sewn closed
   d. they speak eloquently
   e. they speak with false flattery
   f. they speak in elaborate and flowery phrases

_____ 4. When he says that an intellectual would have used "colored propositions," he refers to
   a. purple passages, colors of the spectrum
   b. prejudiced opinions
   c. red, blue, and yellow words

_____ 5. When he says all of the above, he really means that
   a. he will speak like kings, Cardinals, and intellectuals
   b. he will not speak like kings, Cardinals, and intellectuals

_____ 6. What might the underlined phrase in the statement "Every man has *his price*" mean?
   a. his salary
   b. his worth
   c. his vulnerability (weakness)
   d. the bribe he cannot refuse

_____ 7. "Every man has his price" is
   a. always true
   b. sometimes true
   c. rarely true
   d. not true
   Explain your reasoning—

_____ 8. What is a "moral squint"?

    a. nearsightedness

    b. habit of making judgments according to what's right and what's wrong

    c. prejudiced view

    d. farsightedness

    e. viewpoint according to personal values

    f. viewpoint according to objective values

_____ 9. What is a carnivore?

    a. an eater of plants

    b. an eater of meat

_____ 10. What might the phrase in question 9 mean when applied to a human being?

    a. someone out for blood

    b. someone who takes vengeance

    c. someone who hunts for game

    d. someone who would not hesitate to sacrifice another person's life

_____ 11. Amicably means

    a. in love

    b. with spirit

    c. in agreement

    d. in a friendly way

_____ 12. The "breastplate of righteousness" and the "helmet of salvation" refer to

    a. armor for battle

    b. spiritual preparation for spiritual battles

    c. virtues

_____ 13. When he refers to "Old Adam," he is talking about

    a. Everyman

    b. The Common Man

    c. himself

    Explain—

_____ 14. A proposition is

    a. a proposal offered for consideration, acceptance, or adoption

    b. a promise of great things to come

_____ 15. What century does he say is the century for the Common Man?

    a. the sixteenth century

    b. all centuries

_____ 16. What period would be the time for an Uncommon Man? Explain these paradoxical comments about human nature.

    a. "*Great men* get colds in the head just the same as commoners" (act 1).

    b. That man "has plenty of *sense*; he could be *frightened*" (act 1).

    c. That man is "a good son of the Church" (*Churchgoer*). No, he is "a man" (act 1). What is the assumption about human nature in each?

Lesson 5
Dialogue Sequence and Structure

Objectives
- To draw attention to philosophical extremes in two major characters
- To comprehend the content, tone, and continuity of dialogue

Notes to the Teacher

Dialogue challenges the listener-observer to follow the "train of thought" during the repartee in certain scenes of this drama. In the sections of dialogue given in **Handouts 10** and **11**, students' concentration needs to be focused on details of character and theme. Students are required to play detective as they search for clues which will enable them to unscramble the dialogue and rearrange it in the same sequence as found in the text. This will assist students in expanding their knowledge of the characters. These particular excerpts were chosen not only because they are a challenge, but also because they reveal an in-depth analysis of the *characters' traits*: essential elements of *plot* such as the exchange of the silver cup and the need for the pope's dispensation; and *themes* such as the worth of the individual and the private conscience's battle with public duty.

Procedure

1. Distribute **Handouts 10** and **11**. Direct students to work alone on part 1 in both handouts, with texts closed. After a sufficient time, permit students to work with partners. Let them check their accuracy against the text passage in act 1. (Note: pages 1 and 2 of **Handouts 10** and **11** should be duplicated on separate sheets of paper to facilitate side by side reading of the lines.)
   Suggested Responses:
   Handout 10: *AA, L, BB, N, G, F, I, P, M, T, O, D, A, R, U, H, C, B, K, X, E, J, S, CC, W, V, Y, Z, Q.*
   Handout 11: *A, G, O, P, B, E, Q, F, N, R, J, U, AA, CC, H, K, Z, W, D, T, X, M, BB, I, S, C, V, Y, L.*

2. Call students' attention to the "frame" around each episode by looking at the beginning and the end of the dialogues.
   a. In **Handout 10**, the prospect of Rich accepting a teaching position opens the dialogue; at its close, More's advice that he should choose a less politically dangerous career clearly establishes their philosophical differences.
   b. In **Handout 11**, the differences between Wolsey's pragmatic view of the public servant serving his king clashes vividly with More's desires to govern the country by prayer and private conscience.

3. Instruct students to complete part 2 of each handout by carefully explaining the two opposing characters' philosophies based upon the students careful analysis of these passages of dialogue. Tell them to be prepared to support their reasoning in class discussions.

4. A variation to the approach suggested above would be to cut the handout(s) into strips, each containing one line, prior to issuing them to students. Dividing the class into groups would lessen the number of handouts to be cut. It would also facilitate the completion of the activity as well as enhance benefit and enjoyment from it.

Assignment

Finish reading act 1. (You may wish to consult Lesson 6 for an activity to be initiated while students complete the reading of act 1.)

Scrambled Dialogue 1

Part 1

Directions: The following is a scrambled dialogue from the early part of act 1. Number these lines from 1 to 29 in the same order of conversation as they appear in the text. Several of these lines are already numbered correctly to assist you. Refer to the text only when told to do so.

Rich has just asked More if he should call his association with More "acquaintance" or "friendship." More has affirmed "friendship," so Rich expresses surprise that More has not yet put in a good word for him to help get a job. But More has made a contact and at this point announces the open position.

A. _____ *More*: And buy, what?

B. _____ *Rich*: Oh . . . (chagrined) So you give it away, of course.

C. _____ *More*: You'll get several gowns for that I should think. It was sent to me a little while ago by some woman. Now she's put a lawsuit into the Court of Requests. It's a bribe, Richard.

D. _12_ *Rich*: Well—I—Yes, I will.

E. _____ *More*: Well, I'm not going to keep it, and you need it. Of course—if you feel it's contaminated . . .

F. _6_ *Rich*: Beautiful.

G. _____ *More*: A man should go where he won't be tempted. Look, Richard, see this. (He hands him a silver cup.) Look . . . Look . . .

H. _____ *Rich*: I want a gown like yours.

I. _____ *More*: Italian . . . Do you want it?

J. _____ *Rich*: No, no. I'll risk it. (They both smile.)

K. _____ *More*: Yes!

L. _____ *Rich*: What? What post?

M. _____ *More*: No joke; keep it; or sell it.

N. _____ *Rich*: (Bitterly disappointed) A teacher!

O. _____ *More*: You'll sell it, won't you?

P. _____ *Rich*: Why?

Q. _29_ *More*: (Grimly) Be a teacher.

R. _____ *Rich*: (With sudden ferocity) Some decent clothes!

S. _____ *More*: But, Richard, in office they offer you all sorts of things. I was once offered a whole village, with a mill, and a manor house, and heaven knows what else—a coat of arms, I shouldn't be surprised. Why not be a teacher? You'd be a fine teacher. Perhaps even a great one.

T. _____ *Rich*: Well. Thank you, of course. Thank you! Thank you! But—

U. _____ *More*: (With sympathy) Ah.

V. _____ *Rich*: (Laughing) You say that!

W. _____ *More*: You, your pupils, your friends, God. Not a bad public, that . . . Oh, and a quiet life.

X. _20_ *Rich*: To me?

Y. _____ *More*: Richard, I was commanded into office; it was inflicted on me . . . (Rich regards him) Can't you believe that?

Z. _____ *Rich*: It's hard.

AA. __1__ *More*: The Dean of St. Paul's offers you a position; with a house, a servant, and fifty pounds a year.

BB. _____ *More*: At the new school.

CC. _____ *Rich*: And, if I was, who would know it?

Part 2
Discuss the differences in philosophy that are apparent in these two main characters.

Name_____

Date_____

Scrambled Dialogue 2

Part 1

Directions: The following is a scrambled dialogue from the early part of act 1. Number these lines from 1 to 29 in the same order of conversation as they appear in the text. Several of the lines are already numbered correctly to assist you.

More has just arrived at the offices of Cardinal Wolsey in Hampton court. He summoned Sir Thomas to get the latter's answer concerning whether or not he would help Wolsey change the pope's mind, permitting King Henry to divorce Queen Catherine and marry Anne Boleyn.

A. __1__ *Wolsey:* You're a constant regret to me, Thomas. If you could see facts flat on, without that horrible moral squint; with just a little common sense, you could have become a statesman.

B. _____ *Wolsey:* Ach, you're a plodder! Take you altogether, Thomas, your scholarship, your experience, what are you?

C. _____ *Wolsey:* Let him die without an heir and we'll have them back again. Let him die without an heir and this "peace" you think so much of will go out like that! . . . Very well then . . . England needs an heir; certain measures, perhaps regrettable, perhaps not—(pompous) there is much in the Church that needs reformation, Thomas— (More smiles) All right, regrettable! But necessary, to get us an heir! Now explain how you as Councilor of England can obstruct those measures for the sake of your own, private, conscience.

D. _____ *More:* Then clearly all we have to do is approach His Holiness and ask him.

E. __6__ *Wolsey:* . . . Are you going to oppose me? (Trumpet sounds) He's gone in . . . All right, we'll plod. The King wants a son; what are you going to do about it?

F. _____ *Wolsey:* . . . Do you favor a change of dynasty, Sir Thomas? D'you think two Tudors is sufficient?

G. _____ *More:* O, Your Grace flatters me.

H. _____ *More:* There are precedents.

I. _____ *Wolsey:* Then, good night! Oh, your conscience is your own affair; but you're a statesman! Do you remember the Yorkist Wars?

J. _____ *More:* (Steadily) I pray for it daily.

K. _____ *Wolsey:* Yes. All right. Good. Pray. Pray. Pray by all means. But in addition to prayer there is effort. My effort's to secure a divorce. Have I your support or have I not?

L. __29__ *More:* Yes, I should.

M. _____ *Wolsey:* Like that and in other ways—

N. _____ *More:* (Standing up in horrified alarm) For God's sake, Your Grace—

O. _____ *Wolsey:* Don't frivol . . . Thomas, are you going to help me?

P. _____ *More:* (Hesitates, looks away) If Your Grace will be specific.

Q. _____ *More:* (Dry murmur) I'm very sure the King needs no advice from me on what to do about it.

R. _____ *Wolsey:* Then the King needs a son; I repeat, what are you going to do about it?

S. __25__ *More:* Very clearly.

T. __20__ *Wolsey:* I think we might influence His Holiness' answer—

U. _____ *Wolsey:* (Softly) God's death, he means it . . . that thing out there's at least fertile, Thomas.

V. _____ *More*: Well, . . . I believe, when statesmen forsake their own private conscience for the sake of their public duties . . . they lead their country by a short route to chaos . . . And we shall have my prayers to fall back on.

W. _____ *Wolsey*: I don't like plodding, Thomas, don't make me plod longer than I have to—Well?

X. _____ *More*: Like this?

Y. _____ *Wolsey*: You'd like that, wouldn't you? To govern the country by prayer?

Z. _____ *More*: A dispensation was granted so that the King might marry Queen Catherine, for state reasons. Now we are to ask the Pope to dispense with his dispensation, also for state reasons.

AA. _____ *More*: But she's not his wife.

BB. _____ *More*: I've already expressed my opinion on this—

CC. _____ *Wolsey*: No, Catherine's his wife and she's as barren as a brick. Are you going to pray for a miracle?

Part 2

Discuss the differences in philosophy that are apparent in these two main characters.

Lesson 6
Adjectives and Adverbs of Characterization

Objectives

- To promote careful reading of character clues as found in stage directions
- To give students an opportunity to express in writing their evaluation of one of the major characters

Notes to the Teacher

Every word counts! The adjectives and adverbs in stage directions and cues are important in a tightly knit drama. Students must learn that an essential element of any quality work is its artistry of language. In this play, Bolt includes phrases of interpretation for the actors in order to comment on the nature of the characters. By excerpting these adjectives and adverbs and collecting them for their cumulative effect, students will be better able to draw significant conclusions about the motives of and conflicts between the characters. Part 1 of this exercise is most effective if initiated as students begin the study of act 1. Part 2 of this lesson is a helpful evaluation tool after the study of act 1 has been completed.

Procedure

1. Distribute **Handout 12** after the Common Man's opening speech has been studied.

2. Instruct students that at the heading of each column, they must fill in the name of the correct character. They are then to enter additional adjectives and adverbs (even phrases if appropriate) in the correct columns as they discover them during continued close reading of the first act.

3. Ask students which characters they would advise Sir Thomas (or the king) to keep as friends and which they would recognize as enemies. Tell students to be prepared to explain their reasoning.

Suggested Responses:
Column 1
The Steward
Column 2
Norfolk
Column 3
Rich
Column 4
Alice

4. Tell students that once they have completed the study of act 1, they are to proceed to **Handout 13**. Choose one of those characters identified in **Handout 12** and write the two short essays required. The first one will evaluate whether More should or should not trust this character; the second essay will discuss how the student thinks this character will act under pressure. Tell them to include examples in both of their essays to support their reasoning.

Assignment

Read act 2 prior to studying Lesson 7.

Tipped Off By a Word

Directions: Often the stage directions which a playwright gives his actors for the tone of voice, facial expressions, and body movement will give clues to the character's nature.

Using only the stage directions and cues given in act 1, identify the four characters in the columns below. The list has been started for you. Continue adding adjectives and adverbs (including phrases) which you find that describe that character. Do this for all four columns through the completion of your study of act 1. *Remember*: use only stage directions and cues.

Character's Name

1	2	3	4
contemptuously	irritably	enthusiastically	irritably
snubbing	sportsman	bitterly	suspiciously
soapy	slyly	disappointed	hotly
reproachfully	delighted	with sudden ferocity	indignant
	roar	chagrined	

A Man for All Seasons
Lesson 6
Handout 13 (page 1)

Name_____
Date_____

Friend or Foe?

Directions: After you have completed the study of act 1, you will be prepared to make some accurate judgments about the characters. Write two short essays, using one of the discussed characters in **Handout 12**. Follow the instructions for both essays. Include examples to support your reasoning in this exercise.

Essay 1: This paragraph will evaluate whether Sir Thomas More could trust your character or not.

Essay 2: Discuss how you think this character would act under pressure. Give your reasons. Also give examples if the character has done something to support your opinion.

Lesson 7
Literary Quality of Dialogue

Objectives

- To discover the richness and variety of language usage through a comparative study of several passages
- To illustrate how an author reveals the many facets of a character through effective dialogue

Notes to the Teacher

This work of literature is stimulating entertainment and great drama because the author so effectively captures the many dimensions of his characters, especially Sir Thomas More. Robert Bolt designed his main character's speech so artistically that the reader easily sees the many facets of More: lawyer, intellectual, poet, wit, Catholic, statesman, friend, husband, father, and above all, prudent idealist.

This lesson enables students to see the purposes and effects of language through the examination of isolated bits of dialogue.

Procedure

1. Give students these general scenes. You may want to list them on the chalkboard or on an overhead projector.
   - ____ a minor automobile accident at a traffic signal
   - ____ a beautiful summer sunset
   - ____ an athletic event (football, soccer, etc.)
   - ____ a recent movie or TV program

   Ask a student to describe one of the above scenes, talking in the manner of one of the characters listed below, using the language styles associated with him or her. Ask another student to use the same scene but choose a different character to describe the scene.
   - ____ a lawyer
   - ____ a professional athlete
   - ____ a modern teenager
   - ____ a modern salesman
   - ____ a college professor
   - ____ _____
     your choice

2. Distribute **Handout 14**. Ask students what this fencing phrase title could mean as applied to the dialogue of the play. Tell them to begin working on the exercise individually. Remind them that some of the examples could have more than on answer and to list as many correct choices as they can.
   Suggested Responses:
   1. J, K
   2. A, C, F, J
   3. C, F, L
   4. A, F, H, J
   5. B, E, L
   6. B, E, L
   7. B, E, L
   8. B, D, E, L
   9. A, G, K
   10. A, B, C, F, G, H, J
   11. C, F, J
   12. E, G, I, K, L
   13. A, B, D, G, H, J
   14. A, B, D, G, H, J
   15. B, D, F, G, J, L
   16. E, F, G, L
   17. D, F
   18. B, D
   19. A, D, G, L
   20. B, E, F, K

3. After sufficient time has been given, have students in small groups compare interpretations. Tell them that it is not necessary that all members of the group agree but that each student must be able to give a reason for the choice(s) that is (are) satisfactory to the other students(s).

4. Each group might be assigned to find a passage on their own which would correspond to one of the twelve types listed on the handout. In the process of hunting, skimming, and rereading, students can explain challenging passages to one another.

Name_____

Date_____

Parry and Thrust

Directions: Sir Thomas More is a very interesting and highly intelligent character. He is full of surprises, a man of many interests. The versatility and richness of his character are reflected in the dialogue of the play. Mark the following passages as follows:

A. witty
B. philosophical
C. humorous
D. poetic, using images and metaphors
E. logical, using reasoned arguments
F. ironic
G. accurate or true
H. satirical
I. sympathetic
J. insightful, penetrating (reading character)
K. prudent
L. steady, controlled, nonplussed, unruffled

Note: Some passages may have more than one correct answer. List those which you think are accurate.

	More:	O, Your Grace, here's a young man desperate for employment. Something in the clerical line.
	Norfolk:	Well, if you recommend him.
1. _____	*More*:	No. I don't recommend him; but I point him out (act 1, p. 9).
	Wolsey:	More, you should have been a cleric!
2. _____	*More*:	(Amused, Looking down from gallery) Like yourself, Your Grace (act 1, p. 14)?
	Wolsey:	. . . The King wants a son; what are you going to do about it?
3. _____	*More*:	(Dry murmur) I'm very sure the King needs no advice from me on what to do about it (act 1, p. 12).
	More:	(Interested) Buy a man with suffering?
	Rich:	Impose suffering, and offer him—escape.
4. _____	*More*:	Oh. For a moment I thought you were being profound (act 1, p. 4).
	Roper:	I'd cut down every law in England to do that!
5. _____	*More*:	Oh? (Roused and excited) Oh? (Advances on Roper) And when the last law was down, and the Devil turned round on you—where would you hide, Roper, the laws all being flat (act 1, p. 38)?
	Margaret:	Father, that man's bad.
	More:	There is no law against that.
	Roper:	There is! God's law!
6. _____	*More*:	Then God can arrest him (act 1, p. 36).
	Roper:	Sophistication upon sophistication!
7. _____	*More*:	No, sheer simplicity. The law, Roper, the law, I know what's legal, not what's right. And I'll stick to what's legal.
	Roper:	Then you set man's law above God's!

8. _____ *More:* No, far below; but let *me* draw your attention to a fact—I'm *not* God. The currents and eddies of right and wrong, which you find such plain sailing, I can't navigate. I'm no voyager. But in the thickets of the law, oh, there I'm a forester. I doubt if there's a man alive who could follow me there . . . (act 1, p. 37).

9. _____ *More:* Margaret, . . . I'll not have you repeat lawyer's gossip. I'm a lawyer myself and I know what it's worth (act 1, p. 19).

Rich: . . . I'll permit no breath of insolence!

10. _____ *Steward:* (The very idea is shocking) I should hope not, sir. (Exit Rich) Oh, I can manage this one! He's just my size (act 2, p. 61)!

11. _____ *Norfolk:* Good day, Alice. (Going) I'd rather deal with you than your husband (act 2, p. 53).

Alice: In short you don't trust us!

More: . . . I'm the Lord Chief Justice . . . and I take your hand (He does so) and I clamp it on the Bible . . . and I say: "Woman, has your husband made a statement on these matters?" Now—on peril of your soul remember—what's your answer?

Alice: No.

12. _____ *More:* And so it must remain . . . (act 2, pp. 55–56).

13. _____ *More:* The nobility of England, my lord, would have snored through the Sermon on the Mount. But you'll labor like Thomas Aquinas over a rat-dog's pedigree (act 2, p. 71).

14. _____ *More:* And what would you do with a water spaniel that was afraid of water? You'd hang it! Well, as a spaniel is to water, so is a man to his own self (act 2, p. 71).

15. _____ *More:* Death . . . comes for us all, my lords. Yes, even for Kings he comes, to whom amidst all their Royalty and brute strength he will neither kneel or make them any reverence nor pleasantly desire them to come forth, but roughly grasp them by the very breast and rattle them until they be stark dead (act 2, p. 87)!

16. _____ *More:* The maxim of the law is (Very carefully) "Silence gives consent." If, therefore, you wish to construe what my silence "betokened," you must construe that I consented, not that I denied (act 2, p. 88).

Margaret: We sit in the dark because we've no candles. And we've no talk because we're wondering what they're doing to you here.

17. _____ *More:* The King's more merciful than you. He doesn't use the rack.

18. _____ *More:* . . . God made the *angels* to show him splendor as he made animals for innocence and plants for their simplicity. But Man he made to serve him wittily, in the tangle of his mind! Our natural business lies in escaping so let's get home and study this Bill (act 2, p. 73).

Alice: (Hostile) You're content, then, to be shut up here with mice and rats when you might be home with us!

19. _____ *More:* (Flinching) Content? If they'd open a crack that wide (Between finger and thumb) I'd be through it. (To Margaret) Well, has Eve run out of apples (act 2, pp. 81–82)?

20. _____ *Jailer:* (Reasonably) You understand my position, sir, there's nothing I can do; I'm a plain, simple man and just want to keep out of trouble (act 2, p. 85).

Lesson 8
Thunderheads and Silver Linings: Prospects for More and Rich

Objectives
- To illustrate how each scene reflects the deterioration of More's situation
- To trace Richard Rich's progress toward a promising future through his moral decay

Notes to the Teacher
After the class has finished reading the play, it would be helpful to point out the scene divisions and the major steps that each scene contributes to the progress of plot and character development. **Handout 15** will accomplish this and also serve as an outline for ready student reference. The conflicts which More faces, either directly or indirectly, in each of these scenes, progressively establishes the battle lines.

A closer study of the conflicts and characters involved in each scene will also show how Bolt juxtaposes these characters for the purpose of illustrating how More's demise and Rich's rise are inversely proportionate. This will clarify one of the author's major themes, the difference between the courage and integrity of More and the weakness and decay of Rich.

Procedure
1. Distribute **Handout 15**. This exercise will be completed most effectively if you divide the students into groups of five. Tell the groups to assign each member three scenes of the play. Each student is responsible for entering the required information. (Note: Copy these charts on separate pages so that each student of the group will have his or her own set of assigned scenes.) Remind them to create an appropriate title for each scene in column A.

2. Let groups share answers in a class discussion. (See next column for answers.)

3. Point out to students that there is an obvious pairing of similar characters and juxtaposing of foils in act 1. Suggest that Bolt does this to emphasize human qualities important to the play and to foreshadow coming events.

4. Ask students to explain the significance of the play's opening scene pairing Rich with More as juxtaposed to the first act's closing scene coupling Rich with Cromwell. Suggest that the act opens with the two philosophical extremes and ends with the pragmatic view seemingly coming into power.

5. Ask students to examine closely the major characters in each scene of act 1. Ask if they see any commonality between the characters who appear in each, other than More himself. Suggest that each scene presents a new threat of confrontation between More and a different character. This foreshadows that almost all of the characters will desert More in one way or another before the final curtain.
Suggested Responses:
Scene Structure in A Man for All Seasons
Act 1

Scene 1: (3–10)		Rich and More
	3-17	the two philosophical extremes
Scene 2: (10–14)		Wolsey and More
	17-24	two views of the Chancellorship
Scene 3: (14–17)		Cromwell versus
	24-27	Chapuys with More "in the middle"
Scene 4: (17–20)		Roper and More
	27-35	two views of the idealist
Scene 5: (20–25)		Henry and Rich
	35-45	two views of the pragmatist
Scene 6: (25–39)		Henry and More
	45-69	the dilemma presented; family members' reactions
Scene 7: (39–44)		Cromwell and Rich
	69-77	the solution to the dilemma

Act 2

Scene 1: (47–51)		Roper, Chapuys, More
	81-89	three different "Catholics" in action and reaction

Moral Storms

Directions: Locate the scenes in the text according to the page numbers given in the left column. Fill in the blank space in the left column with a *short*, but appropriate title for each scene. Complete the remaining columns by inserting the answers required by the column headings.

A Scenes and titles	B Major characters involved	C Discuss major action or concerns of the scene	D What aspects of More's character are highlighted? Is Rich developed? How?
Act 1 Scene 1 (3–10) _____ _____ _____			
Scene 2 (10–14) _____ _____ _____			Discuss Wolsey's dominant traits.
Scene 3 (14–17) _____ _____ _____			
Scene 4 (17–20) _____ _____ _____			Discuss Ropers's dominant traits.

A Man for All Seasons
Lesson 8
Handout 15 (page 2)

Name_____
Date_____

A	B	C	D
Scenes and titles	Major characters involved	Discuss major action or concerns of the scene	What aspects of More's character are highlighted? Is Rich developed? How?
Scene 5 (20–25) _____ _____ _____			
Scene 6 (25–39) _____ _____ _____			Discuss Henry's dominant traits.
Scene 7 (39–44) _____ _____ _____			
Act 2 Scene 1 (47–51) _____ _____ _____			

A Man for All Seasons
Lesson 8
Handout 15 (page 3)

Name_____

Date_____

A	B	C	D
Scenes and titles	Major characters involved	Discuss major action or concerns of the scene	What aspects of More's character are highlighted? Is Rich developed? How?
Scene 2 (52–57) _____ _____ _____			
Scene 3 (57–61) _____ _____ _____			
Scene 4 (61–65) _____ _____ _____			
Scene 5 (65–69) _____ _____ _____			

A Man for All Seasons
Lesson 8
Handout 15 (page 4)

Name_____
Date_____

A	B	C	D
Scenes and titles	Major characters involved	Discuss major action or concerns of the scene	What aspects of More's character are highlighted? Is Rich developed? How?
Scene 6 (69–73) _____ _____ _____			
Scene 7 (74–79) _____ _____ _____			
Scene 8 (79–85) _____ _____ _____			
Scene 9 (85–93) _____ _____ _____			
Scene 10 (93–95) _____ _____ _____			

Lesson 9
Ladder of Philosophical Extremes

Objectives

- To clarify the terms idealist and pragmatist
- To illustrate the broad philosophical spectrum spanned by the characters
- To emphasize the gulf between the morals of More and Rich

Notes to the Teacher

Students must be guided into an understanding of some of the philosophical considerations underlying this work. Before this can take place, however, they must be able to differentiate between the two opposing philosophies of idealism and pragmatism. These opposing systems of thought are epitomized by More and Rich, respectively. Once students understand the differences between these two concepts, they will be able to see that all of the major characters can be generally placed into one of these two camps. It must be pointed out to students, however, that everyone embraces varying degrees of both of these philosophies. Although no one is either totally idealistic or totally pragmatic, Bolt's protagonist and antagonist come very close to these extremes, with the other characters falling somewhere between.

Procedure

1. Distribute **Handout 16**. Give students an opportunity individually to define the two philosophies both from dictionaries and their own experiences. To insure that they fully grasp the concepts, ask for volunteers to share their examples with the class.
   Suggested Responses:
   Idealist: *One whose behavior or thought is based on a concept of things as they should be or as one would wish them to be*
   Pragmatist: *A person who tests the validity of all concepts by their practical results as opposed to imaginary or visionary goals*

2. Distribute **Handout 17**. Explain that the poems represent "two contrary states of the Human Soul." Ask students to relate the animal symbols to philosophies of life defined in **Handout 16** in answering the handout questions.

Suggested Responses:
1. *The unanswered questions in "The Tiger" suggest an awareness and maturity associated with worldly experience which contrast with the innocence of childhood reflected in "The Lamb."*
2. *Answers may relate the childhood innocence expressed in "The Lamb" to an idealistic view of life, while "The Tiger," seen with the wisdom gained by experience, may be viewed as a pragmatic symbol.*

3. Distribute **Handout 18**. Mention that this activity deals with opposites, called polarities. The pull of opposing poles can create tension between individuals or groups. Use the first set of circles as an example: ideal vs. reality. Next to each circle are three words or phrases that might be associated with the idea. Ask students to suggest their possible associations.

4. Following the sample, students complete the handout following directions 1 and 2. Tell them to continue with step 3 of the directions as soon as they finish the first part.
   Sample idea associations for the poles are:
   2. **innocence:** pure, good, naive
      experience: guilt and sin, responsibility, moral decisions
   3. **individual:** personal, self, alone
      society: laws, group, problems
   4. **religious faith:** prayer, morals, worship
   5. **truth:** integrity, honesty, sincerity
      dishonesty: phoniness, lies, pretending

5. Give the following directions before you divide the class into ten groups of two or three in each group:
   a. Share the results of your handout in the group and fill in any answers which are missing from yours.
   b. While you are sharing, I will assign one of the ten circles to your group.
   c. Find two specific examples from *A Man for All Seasons* in which some character operates from the point of view of your assigned circle.
   d. Briefly explain the examples in the space provided on the handout just below line B.

6. Have each group share its findings with the class, while the rest of the students take down one example for each of the circles.

7. Have each group combine with another group to work on page 1 of **Handout 19**.

8. Tell them to determine by group consensus where each character is to be placed on the chart. Acknowledge that some of the placements may be arbitrary and based on minimal shades of differences. One example of this would be the placement of Chapuys and Cranmer. The students should base their decisions upon examples in the text.

9. Issue **Handout 19**, page 2. You may want to give this as an assignment to be due later. Ask students to follow the directions carefully. Insure that they give a specific example for each label with which they tag the character.

Understanding Philosophies

Directions: Define the two terms. First, use a dictionary or other reference source. Then put that definition into your own words. Use an actual example to illustrate the accuracy of your response. Respond to the last part concerning your experiences.

1. Idealist
   a. Dictionary/reference source

   b. Your example

   c. Explain something you recently did which could be considered as idealistic.

2. Pragmatist
   a. Dictionary/reference source

   b. Your example

   c. Explain something you did recently which could be considered as pragmatic.

Name_____

Date_____

Contrary Souls

Directions: Read the following poems by the eighteenth-century Romantic poet William Blake, whose works were often studies in contrasts. Answer the questions that follow.

The Lamb

Little Lamb, who made thee?
Dost thou know who made thee?
Gave thee life, and bid thee feed,
By the stream and o'er the mead;
Gave thee clothing of delight,
Softest clothing, woolly, bright;
Gave thee such a tender voice,
Making all the vales rejoice?
Little Lamb, who made thee?
Dost thou know who made thee?

Little Lamb, I'll tell thee,
Little Lamb, I'll tell thee:
He is called by thy name,
For He calls Himself a Lamb,
He is meek, and He is mild;
He became a little child.
I a child, and thou a lamb,
We are called by His name.
Little Lamb, God bless thee!
Little Lamb, God bless thee!

The Tiger

Tiger, tiger, burning bright
In the forest of the night,
What immortal hand or eye
Could frame thy fearful symmetry?

In what distant deeps or skies
Burnt the fire of thine eyes?
On what wings dare he aspire?
What the hand dare seize the fire?

And what shoulder, and what art,
Could twist the sinews of thy heart?
When thy heart began to beat,
What dread hand forged thy dread feet?

What the hammer? What the chain?
In what furnace was thy brain?
What the anvil? What dread grasp
Dared its deadly terrors clasp?

When the stars threw down their spears,
And watered heaven with their tears,
Did He smile his work to see?
Did He who made the lamb make thee?

Tiger, tiger, burning bright
In the forest of the night,
What immortal hand or eye
Dare frame thy fearful symmetry?

1. How are the voices in "The Lamb" and "The Tiger" different?

2. "The Lamb" and "The Tiger" are taken from Blake's *Songs of Innocence* and *Songs of Experience.* In combining the two works, he used the subtitle "Showing the Two Contrary States of the Human Soul." In a paragraph or two, compare Blake's contrary states shown in the two poems with the opposing philosophies defined in **Handout 16**.

Beliefs at Odds

Directions:

1. Notice that in each set below, the circle on the left is opposite in meaning from the circle on the right. Each stands for a different way of looking at life.

2. For each numbered blank on line A, write a word or idea that you associate with the nearer circle. The associations can come from your own experiences or from *A Man for All Seasons*.

3. Next, on line B place an "X" at some position along it closer to the circle that shows the way you look at life. Make your decision after some careful, honest thought.

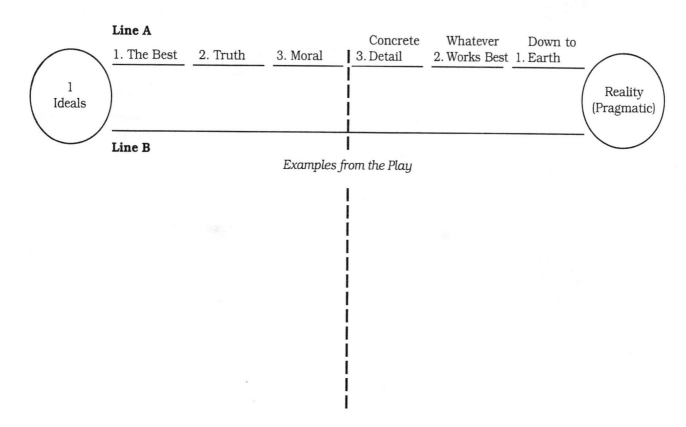

Line A

| 1. The Best | 2. Truth | 3. Moral | 3. Detail (Concrete) | 2. Works Best (Whatever) | 1. Earth (Down to) |

1 Ideals

Reality (Pragmatic)

Line B

Examples from the Play

Name_____
Date_____

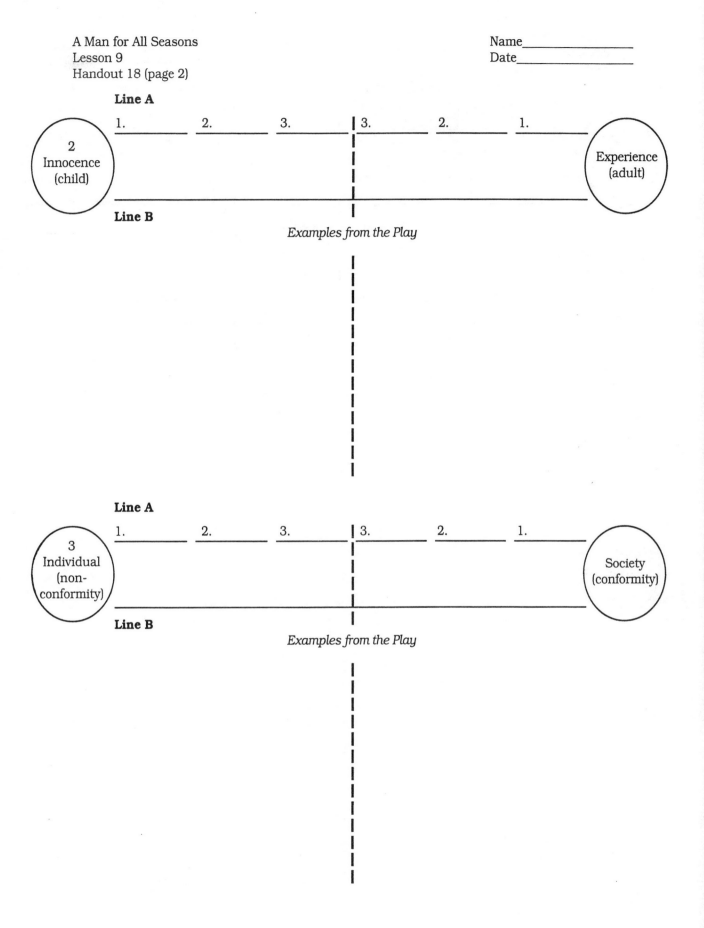

Line A

2 Innocence (child)

1. _____ 2. _____ 3. _____ | 3. _____ 2. _____ 1. _____

Line B

Experience (adult)

Examples from the Play

Line A

3 Individual (non-conformity)

1. _____ 2. _____ 3. _____ | 3. _____ 2. _____ 1. _____

Line B

Society (conformity)

Examples from the Play

Line A

| 1._____ | 2._____ | 3._____ | 3._____ | 2._____ | 1._____ |

4
Religious
Faith

Non-belief

Line B

Examples from the Play

Line A

| 1._____ | 2._____ | 3._____ | 3._____ | 2._____ | 1._____ |

5
Truth

Falsehood

Line B

Examples from the Play

Name_____

Date_____

Ranking the Roles

Directions: Place the characters from the list into column A on the chart according to their philosophy, most idealistic at the top and strongest pragmatist at the bottom. Second, in column B give an example of something the character did or said which justifies the position you chose for him or her.

List

Norfolk
Cranmer
Roper
More
Alice
Margaret
Cromwell
Henry
Chapuys
Rich
Wolsey
Common Man

Column A	Column B—Explanation of Your Ranking	
		Strongest Idealist
		Strongest Pragmatist

Iscariots Away!

It is human nature to try to persuade someone that your beliefs are the correct ones. There are several ways to achieve this goal. You may try to move people through logical arguments. If this does not succeed, you might try playing on their weaknesses through temptation, threats, even subterfuge. The characters in this play attempt to get More to change his mind through some of these methods.

Directions: First, choose one or more of these labels—tempter, betrayer, tormentor—for each of the characters in the chart. For each label you choose, give an example of something said or done which justifies that label.

Name	Examples which explain your choice(s) of label
Norfolk	
Roper	
Alice	
Margaret	
Cromwell	
Wolsey	
Rich	
Common Man	

Lesson 10
Paraphrasing and Imagery:
Seeking Ideas

Objectives
- To establish major ideas from the play by paraphrasing key speeches
- To read dialogue with scrutiny
- To focus attention on poetic devices such as metaphors and to see how these devices enhance major ideas

Notes to the Teachers

Even the most capable students encounter literary passages which are difficult to understand. To fully appreciate good literature, students must be taught how to resolve reading problems. One valuable technique to use is paraphrasing. Assuming that students have taken the time to define words which they did not know, the next step is to put it into their own language. The key to good paraphrasing is to account for all ideas in the passage. Once students feel comfortable with this method of interpreting difficult passages, they must then learn how to recognize which passages are keys to understanding the play. Students are apt to skim over vital sections, not realizing their significance. One way to develop their ability to recognize essential dialogue is to excerpt passages. They can then discuss their value to the overall fabric of the work. Bolt includes thematically important speeches throughout both acts. This lesson requires students to paraphrase several of them in order to see the development of character and the revelation of meaning more clearly.

Another problem that confronts many students is comprehending poetic imagery. Even if they recognize it as a deliberate device, students often are baffled about both the interpretation and its relevance to the larger themes of the work. This lesson gives students practice in recognizing and developing an understanding of metaphors. Bolt says in his introduction to the text.

> I have used a lot of metaphors . . . as a figure for the superhuman context I took the largest, most alien, least formulated thing I know, the sea and water. The references to ships, rivers, currents, tides, navigation, and so on are all used for this purpose.

> Society by contrast figures as dry land . . . But if, as I think, a play is more like a poem than a straight narration . . . then imagery ought to be important.

Students need to be guided into an appreciation of this poetic technique in a genre with which they do not generally associate such devices.

Procedure

1. Distribute **Handout 20**. Insure that the students understand the term *paraphrasing* before directing them to begin the exercise.

2. Divide the class into groups of four. Instruct the groups that one member should be assigned to paraphrase one of the quotations.

3. Having completed the exercise, have groups discuss the paraphrases of each of the quotations. Check for their accuracy and completeness.

4. Issue **Handout 21**. Discuss the definition of the term as stated in the directions.

5. Again divide the class into groups of four. Each member must choose two of the eight terms in the chart and collect three metaphors which illustrate each.

6. Ask the class to share examples and responses to the exercise at the bottom of the chart. Share Bolt's remarks about the metaphors with the class.
   Suggested Responses:
   ships: *Chapuys and Cromwell (pg. 22)*
   More (pg. 73)
   water: *Common Man (pg. 25)*
   More (pg. 19)
   More (pg. 38)
   navigation: *Henry (pg.29)*
   More (pg. 38)
   fishing: *Cromwell (pg. 60)*
   land: *More (pg. 38)*
   hunting: *Norfolk and Alice (pg. 7)*
   forest: *More (pp. 37–38)*
   animals: *Norfolk and Alice (pg. 7)*
   Norfolk and Alice (pp. 71–73)

61

Saying It for Every Man

When reading literature, you may sometimes encounter a passage which may not be very clear at first. If you rewrite that section in your own words, you have to work it out in a careful, logical way. This process is called paraphrasing. It will help you come to a clearer understanding of the author's meaning.

Directions: Read carefully the sections of dialogue below. Then choose one passage and on your paper, paraphrase it. Write it as though you were explaining it to a friend who had never read it. Be sure to include all portions of the passage. You may refer to the dictionary.

Quotation 1

COMMON MAN: The great thing's not to get out of your depth . . . What I can tell them is common knowledge! But now they've given money for it and everyone wants value for his money. They'll make a secret of it now to prove they've not been bilked . . . They'll make it a secret by making it dangerous . . . Mm . . . Oh, when I can't touch the bottom I'll go deaf, blind and dumb. (He holds out coins.) And that's more than I earn in a fortnight (act 1, pp.24–25)!

Quotation 2

MORE: No, sheer simplicity. The law, Roper, the law. I know what's legal not what's right. And I'll stick to what's legal . . . let me draw your attention to a fact— I'm not God. The currents and eddies of right and wrong, which you find such plain sailing, I can't navigate. I'm no voyager. But in the thickets of the law, oh, there I'm a forester. I doubt if there's a man alive who could follow me there, thank God . . . What would you do? Cut a great road through the law to get after the Devil? . . . And when the last law was down, and the Devil turned round on you—where would you hide, Roper, the laws all being flat? This country's planted thick with laws from coast to coast—man's laws, not God's—and if you cut them down—and you're just the man to do it—d'you really think you could stand upright in the winds that would blow then? . . . I'd give the Devil benefit of law, for my own safety's sake . . . And whoever hunts for me. Roper, God or Devil, will find me hiding in the thickets of the law! And I'll hide my daughter with me! Not hoist her up the mainmast of your seagoing principles! They put about too nimbly (act 1, pp. 37–38)!

Quotation 3

MORE: Hear me out. You and your class have 'given in'—as you rightly call it—because the religion of this country means nothing to you one way or the other . . . The nobility of England, my lord, would have snored through the Sermon on the Mount. But you'll labor like Thomas Aquinas over a rat-dog's pedigree. Now what's the name of those distorted creatures you're all breeding at the moment? . . . What's the name of those dogs? Marsh mastiffs? Bog beagles? . . . And what would you do with a water spaniel that was afraid of water? You'd hang it! Well, as a spaniel is to water, so is a man to his own self. I will not give in because I oppose it—I do—not my pride, not my spleen, nor any other of my appetites but *I* do—*I!* . . . Is there no single sinew in the midst of this that serves no appetite of Norfolk's but is just Norfolk? There is! Give *that* some exercise, my lord (act 2, pp. 71–72)!

Quotation 4

MORE: When a man takes an oath, Meg, he's holding his own self in his own hands. Like water. And if he opens his fingers *then*—he needn't hope to find himself again. Some men aren't capable of this, but I'd be loathe to think your father one of them.

MARGARET: In any State that was half good, you would be raised up high, not here, for what you've done already. It's not your fault the State's three-quarters bad. Then if you elect to suffer for it, you elect yourself a hero.

MORE: That's very neat. But look now . . . If we lived in a State where virtue was profitable, common sense would make us good, and greed would make us saintly. And we'd live like animals or angels in the happy land that *needs* no heroes. But since in fact we see that avarice, anger, envy, pride, sloth, lust, and stupidity commonly profit far beyond humility, chastity, fortitude, justice and thought, and have to choose, to be human at all . . . why then perhaps we must stand fast a little—even at the risk of being heroes (act 2, p. 81).

Name_____

Date_____

Meaning through Metaphor

Writers often use symbolic language to emphasize an idea which is central to the literature. The authors will not tell you directly what this theme is but rather imply it through such devices as metaphors. A metaphor is defined as a figure of speech in which there is an implied comparison between two dissimilar objects, such as the Shakespearean line. "All the world's a stage . . . " Politicians refer to their governments as "*ships* of state" implying that everyone from the head of state to the individual voter has certain specific responsibilities to perform in order to keep the government running effectively, not allowing it to "*sink*."

Directions:

1. Complete the chart below by finding examples in the text that will match the items listed in column A. Enter at least three matching images in column B by paraphrasing the quote from which the example was taken.

2. After you have completed the chart, study the examples you have entered. Try to find a contrast between the two sets of images. Write a statement expressing what both the sea and land metaphors might represent.

Metaphors Related to the Sea		Metaphors Related to the Land	
Column A	Column B—Matching Examples	Column A	Column B—Matching Examples
Ships	1. 2. 3.	Land	1. 2. 3.
Water	1. 2. 3.	Hunting	1. 2. 3.
Navigation	1. 2. 3.	Forest	1. 2. 3.
Fishing	1. 2. 3.	Animals	1. 2. 3.

Lesson 11
Title as Theme

Objectives

- To show the relationship between the title of this play and the many qualities of its main character
- To categorize all the members of the cast into the four types identified by Bolt's character, King Henry

Notes to the Teacher

Students must realize when they analyze a quality work of literature that the title often gives valuable clues about major aspects of both the characters and themes. Once they have discovered this vital relationship, they can uncover many rich insights which will make the study of the work all the more rewarding.

This lesson is designated for students to examine this relationship and to help them see how Bolt juxtaposes Sir Thomas More with all the other characters through King Henry's evaluation of the subjects of his realm.

Procedure

1. Distribute **Handout 22**. Ask students to respond to part 1.
   Suggested Responses:
   A fair-weather friend is a person who seems to be your close ally when things are going well; however, when you have misfortunes, this person will not stand by you with assistance and comfort. He or she will not put forth any effort or have compassion for you.

2. Instruct students to continue to part 2 of the handout.
   Suggested Responses:
   1. honest lawyer-judge
   2. faithful Catholic
   3. comforting husband
   4. protective father
   5. loyal friend
   6. lover of life
   7. true gentleman
   8. polite wit
   9. prudent idealist
   10. intellectual philosopher

3. Direct the class to proceed to part 3 of the handout.

Suggested Responses:
1. Richard Rich
2. King Henry
3. Duke of Norfolk
4. William Roper
5. various Common Man roles (others are possibilities)

4. Inform students that they are to write a response for part 4 which contains examples from the text.
   Suggested Response:
   Guide students to see that More is the very opposite of the fair-weather friend. No matter what the climate, he will not sway from his principles, change his allegiances, nor alter his personality.

5. Let students compare their short essays with other students. Ask for volunteers to read their essays. You may want to discuss the following quotations as they relate to students' essays.

   The text gives, as epigraphs. the two quotes:

   > More is a man of an angel's wit and singular learning; I know not his fellow. For where is the man of that gentleness, lowliness, and affability? And as time requireth a man of marvellous mirth and pastimes; and sometimes of as sad gravity: a man for all seasons.
   > —Robert Whittinton

   > He was the person of the greatest virtue these islands ever produced.
   > —Samuel Johnson

6. Distribute **Handout 23**. Instruct students to put the names missing from the quotation at the top of the appropriate column in the chart. Then list all the other characters as directed.
   A. *Norfolk* — *Chapuys*
   — *Attendant*
   B. *Cromwell* — *Rich*
   — *Wolsey*
   — *Cranmer*
   C. *A Mass* — *all of the roles played by the Common Man*
   D. *More* — *Margaret*
   — *Ropert (?)*
   — *Alice (?)*

A Man for All Seasons
Lesson 11
Handout 22 (page 1)

Name_____

Date_____

Wanted: No Fair-Weather Friend

Part 1
Directions: In the space below, explain your concept of a *fair-weather friend*.

Part 2
Directions: Identify as many qualities as you can which describe Sir Thomas More. Give an example to illustrate each one.

1. _____ : _____

2. _____ : _____

3. _____ : _____

4. _____ : _____

5. _____ : _____

6. _____ : _____

7. _____ : _____

8. _____ : _____

9. _____ : _____

10. _____ : _____

A Man for All Seasons
Lesson 11
Handout 22 (page 2)

Name_____
Date_____

Part 3

Directions: Notice the contrast between the qualities which you gave in part 1 and those listed for More in part 2. List five characters from the play that you would characterize as *fair-weather friends*.

1.

2.

3.

4.

5.

Part 4

Directions: Based upon your response thus far, write a short essay below explaining how the title of the play relates to Sir Thomas More.

Name_____

Date_____

Lion-Followers: Jackals and Other Carnivores

Directions: Fill in the correct names in the passage below. Also, transfer those names to the chart. During King Henry's visit to Chelsea, he described to Sir Thomas four kinds of people in his realm:

"There are those like _____ who follow me because I wear the
(also put in Column A below)

crown, and there are those like _____ who follow me because they are
(Column B below)

jackals with sharp teeth and I am their lion, and there is _____ that
(Column C below)

follows me because it follows anything that moves—and there is _____ .
(Column D below)

(Refer to pages 31–32 of the text.)

Directions: In this chart, place all of the other characters listed in the cast into their appropriate column. They should be listed under the characters they most closely resemble. Omit King Henry as he does not fit into any of these categories.

Column A	Column B	Column C	Column D
Name:	Name:	Name:	Name:

Lesson 12
The Modern Choragos: The Common Man

Objectives
- To examine the six roles played by the Common Man
- To compare the Common Man to the Choragos of the Greek tragedies
- To analyze how the Common Man develops themes central to the play

Notes to the Teacher

Bolt's modern play draws obvious parallels between the sixteenth-century tragic situation and those depicted in ancient Greek tragedies. In doing so, however, his Common Man reverses the traditional role which the Greeks gave their Choragos. Bolt has also redefined the character of the traditional tragic hero. By subtle manipulation of these ancient stock figures in his modern setting, he makes clear the themes which are central to the play.

For the people of ancient Greece, going to the theater was a most solemn religious experience with all the ritualistic grandeur and mystery of a high mass. Plays were produced only once or twice annually; therefore, each occasion held special importance. The playwrights came from the ranks of philosophers and teachers. Their works dealt with heroic matters: fate, death, and guilt, as well as the duel between reason and blind passion. The Greek view of the good life was based on a sense of the completeness of one's intellect and the moderation of one's passions, which must be controlled and tempered by reason. The main figure, the tragic hero, was a person of noble birth who held a most significant position in the society but also possessed a fatal flaw, which was usually interpreted as an excess of pride. The Greeks called this weakness *hubris*. Historically, the audience felt deep anguish and pity for this larger-than-life character, but Bolt's tragic figure, Henry, usually attracts the opposite reaction.

When measured by the standard Greek requisites of high position in society and moral collapse through self-serving pride, it is Bolt's King Henry and the followers, not More, who loom as the tragic figures. It is their blind passion for power which has executed a man of faith and integrity. Yet, we feel no awesome sense of remorse for them since our anguish is for the innocent More.

It appears that Bolt has chosen to tilt the traditional tragic world in order to dump it into the audience's lap. To make us aware of this shift of guilt from the good but flawed tragic hero onto the audience is the purpose of the character portrayal of The Common Man. This role is an adaptation of an ancient Greek role, that of a Choragos, the leader and member of the chorus.

The Choragos was a late Sophoclean innovation; the new character's role was to lead the twelve-member chorus. This body of actors was placed between the elevated stage and the audience. Their semicircular area was called the orchestra and contained the altar used to dedicate the event to Dionysus, the Greek god of drama. This group provided rhythmic commentary to the story. It exulted, mourned, dispensed wisdom, foretold dire events, provided the retrospect, and generally kept the drama alive with its flowing poetry, which the Greeks loved. It also functioned as a bridge between the actors on stage and the audience by interpreting events and generalizing the meaning of the action. It often conversed with and gave advice to the actors.

The major function of the chorus was to represent the solemn, elderly seers of the Greek city-states who often attempted to give wise counsel to the tragic hero on how best to come to terms with the divine order of his universe and to lead the "good Greek life."

Bolt says concerning his adaptation of this device:

> . . . [He is] an actor who addresses the audience and comments on the action. But I had him address the audience in character, that is, from within the play. He is intended to draw the audience into the play, not thrust them off . . . He is called "The Common Man" (just as there is a character called "The King") and the word "common" was intended primarily to indicate "that which is common to us all." . . . he was intended to be something with which everyone would be able to identify.

But his Common Man is a caricature of the Greek Choragos. Rather than embodying a solemn tone, his is satiric. Rather than issuing spiritual wisdom to a tragic hero, he wisecracks advice to the audience on how to survive. The ultimate concern here is to save one's skin, even at the expense of the soul. This character has no character. He either makes light of serious situations, evades the issues altogether, or runs away from them claiming he would rather "be a live rat than a dead lion." He is intended to indict us all by his lowly actions since he is to be that which is "common to us all." Contrasting him to the traditional Choragos, we can see that Bolt has turned the world topsy-turvy. He is striving to make the audience conscious of its own short-comings. The Common Man and all of his guises produces the effect Bolt wishes, that is, to make us feel uneasy about the kind of moral world we have created. We identify with him because we see so much of his philosophy shaping our own lives. Therefore, he makes us realize that we, too, have been responsible for the death of More, the man of conscience. Hopefully, we will see in ourselves the Common Man's flaw of self-centeredness. How close do we come to embodying the ancient Greeks' "hubris"?

Thus, paralleling the purpose of traditional Greek tragedy, Bolt's drama gives *us*, not the stock character on stage, but the opportunity of undergoing a true catharsis, "a purging; an emotional purification or relief, usually by sharing in the experience of another" (*Webster's Dictionary*).

Procedure

1. Share with the class the information about the tragic figure and the Choragos.

2. Issue **Handout 24**, page 1. Divide the class into groups of three. For part 1, tell each member of the group to choose two roles of the Common Man to expedite the task.
   Suggested Responses:
   Part 1 asks students to "see the transition from friend to executioner and comment on the 'moral condition' of the Common Man."

   Common Man wears six hats:
   1. *Steward— Both turn away from him after having once befriended him; one knew*
   2. *Boatman— how well, the other only casually (but enough) (More had been kind to both.)*

   3. *Innkeeper—involved in the "entrapment" of More*
   4. *Jailer*
   5. *Juryman— causes his death*
   6. *Hangman*

3. Have students complete part 2.
   Suggested Response:
   Just as we see the seriousness of More's situation becoming worse, the further the plot develops, so, too, do we see the Common Man's role paralleling those who surround him. He becomes swept up in an active role in the condemnation and execution.
   Lead students to understand in depth the following roles of the Common Man.

   The transition:
   The Common Man is first a friend and helper;
   (steward)
   then secondly he is a passive observer and
   (innkeeper)
   then active observer;
   (jailer)
   thirdly, he is the condemner
   (foreman)
   and finally executioner.
   (headsman)

4. Distribute **Handout 24**, part 3. Read through the prefatory information with the class. Then have them respond to the directions.

5. Issue **Handout 25**. Divide the class into groups of five. Tell each member to take a different function to develop.
   Suggested Responses:
   First Example
   1. *page 20—Wolsey's death, More becomes chancellor*
   2. *page 3—foreshadows reactions of Common Man*
   3. *page 3—opening remarks*
   4. *page 10—about More's integrity*
   5. *pages 24–25—after accepting fee for information on More*
   Second Example
   1. *page 47—comments opening act 2*
   2. *page 74—tells fates of several characters*
   3. *page 17—boatman discusses fares*
   4. *pages 39–40—comments about More's education*
   5. *pages 56–57—comments about More's bad luck*

Hats for a Common Man

Part 1

Directions: In column A, list the six roles which the Common Man plays, in chronological order. In column B, explain his relationship with Sir Thomas More. In column C, give a quotation which describes the Common Man's attitude toward the situation in that scene.

A. Title	B. Relationship to More	C. Quote from Scene

Part 2

Directions: What changes in the relationship to More do these roles of the Common Man reveal? (Hint: At first, he is close to More.)

Fedoras for Moderns

Part 3

Robert Bolt wrote, "The action of this play ends in 1535, but the play was written in 1960, and if, in production, one date must obscure the other, it is 1960 which I wish clearly to occupy the stage. The 'Life' of a man like Thomas More proffers a number of caps which in this or any other century we may try on for size."

Directions: Explain what Bolt means by "caps which . . . we may try on for size." It is obvious from his comments that Bolt wrote the play to speak to us today, to make us think about how we would act if we were put into the same positions as the Common Man was.

Directions: First, name three "hats" you wear. (One might be that of a "student.") Then, explain briefly a situation which tested whether or not you would do the right thing.

Hat 1   Situation

Hat 2   Situation

Hat 3   Situation

Name_____

Date_____

Functions of the Common Man

Bolt patterns his Common Man after the chorus and its leader, the Choragos, in the ancient Greek tragic dramas. This group of actors had several jobs during the play:

1. to give historical background to the story
2. to foretell events that were to come later
3. to introduce comic relief into the otherwise serious drama
4. to comment on the character involved
5. to give advice to the audience

Directions: In the chart below, give two examples of the Common Man fulfilling each function listed above.

	First Example	Second Example
1		
2		
3		
4		
5		

Lesson 13
Themes and Perspectives

Objectives
- To examine major ideas as keys to a deeper understanding
- To present several activities which give students a variety of experiences to enhance understanding

Notes to the Teacher

One major purpose for studying literature is to help students relate the ideas and struggles encountered therein to themselves and their times. This play can make an impact upon students once they realize that, although More lived more than four-and-a-half centuries ago, the same battles that he waged are present in their world today. Most teenagers do not undergo trials which are as severe, but they can identify with the persecution of one who thinks he or she is right. Students are quick to react to situations which they perceive as being unfair. They tend to see the world chiefly in terms of right and wrong, light and dark, good and evil. This play's major character easily falls into the category of the "right, light, and good" hero. One of the major challenges in teaching this play, however, is to get some students to realize that there are people today who die for their personal beliefs. Once examples are given (refer to any examples in procedure 5), they will realize that the issue is relevant. Examples of beliefs to which they are committed can then be drawn from personal experiences. Such examples can be the subject of lively classroom discussions. The legality of the draft for military service, the equal rights amendment, and the registration or banning of handguns are a few timely emotional issues that will stir students to express their views.

Discussion of another aspect of the play will involve students in a second major issue. Present the question, "Do the ends justify the means?" Cromwell and Rich would answer affirmatively. This is the major tenet upon which they finally based their actions to dispose of Sir Thomas. Students will have little difficulty discussing the question as it applies to the play but to bring this significant concept into relevance may cause some problems. Pose this situation: "John is a high school senior and has been accepted by one of the nation's major medical schools. His life's goal has always been to become a medical missionary. His acceptance to the college, however, is dependent upon his getting an A in advanced biology. Because of his lack of studying, he has a B before taking the final exam. Only an A on the test will assure him of admittance to medical school. Not enough time remains to study all the necessary notes and materials to prepare for the exam. The only option open to John is to cheat. Should he cheat to gain his dream of helping others, or should he preserve his integrity and conscience and be willing to accept his fate?" This type of open-ended question can spawn other similar ones which will cause the students to examine their own value systems.

Thus, an intensive study of a quality work of literature such as *A Man for All Seasons* will make drawing depth of meaning from it rewarding for both students and teachers alike.

Procedure

Listed below are suggested projects which will extend the drama's major themes beyond the text itself. Some will require more than one class period.

1. Divide the class into small groups. Instruct students to collaborate in the writing of an imaginary scene taking place after the trial but before More's execution. The two main characters are King Henry and Sir Thomas. The purpose of their meeting is up to the writers, but it will not alter the fact that More is to be executed. Remind students that Henry and Thomas had been good friends for many years, that Henry does not have a conscience, as Cromwell confirmed in act 1. Have them consider such questions as the following: What would they discuss? What would Henry have to say about the situation? How would More respond? Tell students that they must keep their characterizations and facts faithful to the text. After the scripts have been completed, let several students enact them. Have the class respond by discussing the issues involved, the textual accuracy, and the groups' creativeness.

2. Set up a debate. Three possible approaches include the following:

a. Divide the class into an even number of small groups. Pair the groups. Each pair will be given the same proposition to debate. Each proposition would have a pro and a con group. This will enhance class interest as the nondebating groups will sit in judgment.

b. Give the same propositions to all of the small groups. After they have become familiar with it, ask for two volunteer groups or choose the two most capable groups to debate the issue while the other groups judge the winning side.

c. Divide the class in half. Issue the proposition and have students hold the debate with you being the judge.

Debate Topics

—No American has the right to oppose the decisions or disobey the laws of his duly-elected government."

—From the Common Man: "Better a live rat than a dead lion."

—"Henry VIII is ultimately responsible for the death of More."

3. Have capable students relate the themes of *A Man for All Seasons* to other important literary works. They could profitably read other works dealing with individuals facing comparable moral dilemmas. Such literature includes Plato's *Apology*, Sophocles' *Antigone*, Shaw's *St. Joan*, Anouilh's *Becket*, Eliot's *Murder in the Cathedral*, Ibsen's *Enemy of the People*, and Miller's *All My Sons* and *The Crucible*.

4. Assign students research projects which require that they compare the moral crisis in the play with real-life dilemmas and historical ethical issues.

5. Research modern martyrs, i.e., Martin Luther King, Jr., Gandhi, present day martyrs in South Africa, Afghanistan, Latin America, the Middle East, Eastern bloc countries, etc.

Conscience and the Crown

He was born, this "man for all seasons," just over 500 years ago in London on Milk Street. Later, in something of a celestial pun, Thomas Fuller was to proclaim him "the brightest star that ever shined in that via lactea."

Sir Thomas More's origins were humble, of "no famous family, but of honest stock," as he wrote in his epitaph for a tomb which, in the end, he never occupied. His father, eventually a knight and a judge, was no more than butler to Lincoln's Inn at the time he advised his young son to study law. Although little in his background prepared him for a political career, save an unwavering moral conviction, a dubious asset at best in such an arena, Thomas More followed his father's urgings and emerged as the Lord Chancellor of Great Britain—and, eventually, a martyred saint.

The intelligence, wit, and spirituality that conspired to propel young More to such dizzying heights and a tumultuous fall were manifested early. While being educated in the household of the Archbishop of Canterbury, he would improvise parts for himself in Christmas pageants, much to the amusement of fellow students. At the age of fourteen, he was sent to Oxford and attended Canterbury College and Christ Church. Fluent in classical languages, he took enormous delight in translating Greek epigrams into Latin. His interest in the theology attracted him to the devotional life of a monk, and for four years, he lived at the London Charterhouse. However, his vows were interrupted by his decision to marry, a decision not easy to make, as he indicated years later in letters from the Tower of London to Margaret, his daughter by his first wife. Throughout his life, he nevertheless retained the austere habits of the Charterhouse: eating and sleeping sparingly, meditating and praying frequently, and, ironically, wearing a hair shirt next to his skin.

In 1504, at the age of twenty-six, Thomas More entered Parliament. One of his first acts was to urge a decrease in appropriations for King Henry VII, a move which naturally infuriated the volatile monarch and dramatically foreshadowed future struggles between More's conscience and the Crown. In revenge, Henry imprisoned More's father and fined and forced Thomas, himself, to withdraw from public office. More then continued to practice law quietly until the death of Henry VII five years later when he resumed public office and was appointed Under-Sheriff of London. At that time, his discourses on such novel concepts as education and rights for women brought him to the attention of the young King Henry VIII.

On Evil May Day of 1515, More helped to restrain a rioting mob of London apprentices, who were attacking foreign merchants. The event was sufficiently noteworthy to be celebrated in an Elizabethan play, *Sir Thomas More*, to which Shakespeare contributed More's speeches on order and authority. Soon, the novice Under-Sheriff was delegated to settle trade disputes in Calais, appointed a member of the King's Council, and finally made Master of Requests.

Thomas More's literary pursuits during this period of his life were, alone, of sufficient brilliance to merit him the immortality later bestowed upon him by martyrdom. While ambassador to Flanders, he wrote the world-famous *Utopia*, his satiric damnation of the "unreasonable polity of Christian Europe, divided by self-interest and greed." With scathing wit, More outlined the mythical pagan and communist state of Utopia, in which all action is governed by reason, and communal interest is the only cure against egoism. For his material, he had drawn on Amerigo Vespucci's descriptions of the new world and on Plato, Pliny, and other classical writers. *Utopia* was such a logical and inspired affirmation of communism that today, there is even a Thomas More room in the Kremlin, paradoxically honoring a Christian saint.

More's ascent to the highest echelons of political power was mercurial. At forty-three, he was knighted. He was appointed Under-Treasurer. At forty-five, he was chosen Speaker of the House of Commons. He was made Chancellor of the Duchy of Lancaster. And, in 1529, when the venal Cardinal Wolsey fell from power, More succeeded him as Lord Chancellor, just as King Henry VIII was seeking an annulment of his marriage to Catherine of Aragon. His fate was sealed.

Unlike the corpulent and corrupt Wolsey, More ruled as Lord Chancellor with justice and charity. A confirmed foe of heresy, he dealt sternly, but never violently, with heretics. The king frequently sought out his company with affection and engaged him in seemingly endless debates of intellect. As the first commoner and the first layman to hold the office of Lord Chancellor, More presided over, but was allowed no vote in, the House of Lords. In that capacity, he introduced the matter of the king's divorce to Parliament, himself abstaining from comment and offering, instead, a dozen learned opinions from various European Universities. While the Pope delayed judgment, the tide of Protestant-ism engulfed England, leaving Thomas More to hold his torch alone against a rising sea. When articles were placed before the convocation of Canterbury effectively depriving the Church of its power to act without the king's consent, Sir Thomas More resigned as Lord Chancellor, pleading reasons of health, "a sharp and constant pain in the chest."

The passion of Saint Thomas was enacted against a pageant of conviction and coercion, promises and perjury, sinners and saints. The Act in Restraint of Appeals severed judicial links between England and Rome. Thomas Cranmer, the new Archbishop of Canterbury, declared the king's first marriage void, and Anne Boleyn was crowned queen. After several frivolous accusations failed to indict More, he was called to appear at court and confirm by oath the Act of Succession, which validated Anne Boleyn's position as queen. With her title, he had no disagreement for the woman had been legally crowned. He refused the oath, however, because it entailed a repudiation of papal supremacy. On April 17, 1533, Sir Thomas More was imprisoned in the Tower of London.

During his incarceration, More continued to write, notably a striking series of letters to his family and friends. Deprived of paper and pen, he was ultimately forced to scrawl his last moving letters of farewell with a piece of charcoal. He was indicted on four counts: his refusal to affirm the king's supremacy, two counts concerning certain correspondence with the Bishop of Rochester while both were imprisoned, and his denial that Parliament could declare the king head of the Church. His defense on the last three counts was allowed, but, because of legal technicalities, his stand on the first faltered. He claimed that, by remaining silent on all pertinent issues, he had not spoken against the supremacy, and that, by common law, silence implies consent. The jury refused this logic, and, on the perjured testimony of Richard Rich, he was condemned to death.

On July 7, 1535, Sir Thomas More was beheaded. On the very scaffolding itself, he broke his cherished silence and proclaimed the famous words, "I die the king's good servant, but God's first."

His body was buried in the chapel of St. Peter in the Tower. His head was placed on London Bridge and was reported to have been thrown into the river. However, the discovery of a head in the vault of his daughter, Margaret Roper, in 1824 has led to the current belief that his beloved Meg bartered for his remains and carried them with her to her own final resting.

His story has never been laid to rest. This passionate history, such a tale of irrevocable conviction, inspired many retellings, but few as eloquent as Robert Bolt's *A Man for All Seasons*. Like More himself, Bolt once amused students with his impoverished Christmas pageants. The germ of an extraordinary talent matured, and soon Robert Bolt became known as one of the most promising playwrights in the English language. *A Man for All Seasons* grew out of a television drama that was commissioned by the British Broadcasting Corporation in 1953. Extended to a full stage version, the play enjoyed an overwhelming success in London seven years later. Opening on Broadway on Thanksgiving Eve, 1961, the ecstatic American reviews for the play were virtually ignored in the midst of holiday festivities but word of mouth soon sparked business and the play ran in New York for a phenomenal 637 performances. It was honored with eight Tony Awards and the New York Drama Critics' Circle Award. When adapted to the screen, the film version garnered an incredible eight nominations and six Academy Awards, including one for Bolt's screenplay and another for Best Picture.

And so, five hundred years after his inauspicious birth, the life of Sir Thomas More continues to perplex and to inspire—to reaffirm the still, small voice of conscience against the roar of oppression. No man of any age better merits the tribute paid him by a London schoolteacher in 1520, years before he was on the brink of glory: "More is a man of an angel's wit and singular learning; a man of marvelous mirth and pastimes, and sometimes of sad gravity, as one might say, a man for all seasons."

—James H. Hansen

Oral Report Topics

This can be used to have students present a brief, yet in-depth, discussion of segments of the text. Each presentation would take five to seven minutes. Students may develop presentations according to the information required on the accompanying outline which could also be used as a grading guide.

1. pp. 4–6 (top half) and p. 8 (top half)
2. pp. 11–14 (top half)
3. pp. 17–20
4. pp. 21–25 (top half)
5. pp. 29–33
6. pp. 34–35
7. pp. 36–39
8. pp. 40–44
9. p. 47 (bottom half)–p. 51
10. pp. 52–54 (top half)
11. p. 54 (bottom half)–p. 55
12. pp. 56–57 (top half)
13. p. 57 (bottom half)–p. 61
14. p. 61 (bottom half)–p. 63, plus Chapuy's speech, top of p. 64
15. pp. 64–65 (to Cromwell's speech)
16. p. 65 (begin with Cromwell's speech)–p. 69 (to Cromwell's exit)
17. p. 69 (at bottom of page)–p. 73 (top half)
18. pp. 75–79
19. pp. 80–85 (top half); look closely at major speeches on p. 81
20. pp. 86–90
21. pp. 91–95
22. Discuss Common Man's speech on pages 94–95 and how it refers to major ideas in the play. How does it apply to "ordinary" (common) modern people? What reaction are we supposed to have to it, and why?

Oral Report Form

Name _____

Page numbers of presentation _____

1. Plot development

2. Setting significance

3. Character developments

4. Poetic devices—symbols, metaphors, allusions, etc.

5. Important words, phrases, etc. to be defined

6. Thematic developments

Tests

Act 1

1. Explain what More does with the silver goblet. *Why* does he do it?

2. Why does Wolsey send for More to meet with him?

3. Explain why More is opposed to Margaret marrying Roper? Why is this such a major issue with More?

4. For whom is Chapuys working, or (to put it another way) what does he want More to do?

5. Cromwell meets someone in a tavern in the last scene of this act. Who is it? What is the purpose of the meeting? How does this scene foreshadow events in Act 2?

Name_____

Date_____

Act 2

1. How does the book entitled *A Defense of the Seven Sacraments* play a role in one of the "inquiries" through which More must go?

2. More and Norfolk finally depart from one another not the best of friends. Explain what happens to cause the split in their friendship. Why does it happen?

3. What was the "Act of Succession"? Explain why More would not sign it.

4. More says to Meg during the visit to him in the Tower's cell. "The King's more merciful than you. He doesn't use the rack." Explain how Meg was cruel to him during this visit.

5. Explain the role Rich plays in More's final trial scene; be specific.

Essay Writing Topics

1. Normally, the weapons of our heroes in both fact and fiction are the conventional ones: firearms, swords, etc. Write a paper in which you discuss the weapons of Sir Thomas More which arm him against the efforts and schemes of Henry and his regime.

2. Many of society's heroes are characterized by their tremendous physical strength, romantic appeal, and/or valor in battle. Write a paper which emphasizes that Sir Thomas More is a rather unique hero since he was not a physically robust figure, slew no "dragons," and was certainly not a romantic figure who appealed to fair maidens throughout England.

3. It has been stated that the Common Man is "the most direct representative of the audience (the 'mass that follows') and that he indicts (condemns or points an 'accusing finger') by his own actions those people of any age who set self-interest above all other values." Show how this is a valid statement.

4. Robert Whittinton once said:

   > More is a man of an angel's wit and singular learning; I know not his fellow. For where is the man of that gentleness, lowliness, and affability? And as time requireth a man of marvelous mirth and pastimes; and sometimes of as sad gravity: a man for all seasons.

   Write a paper which analyzes the meaning of the *title*, using various attributes, beliefs, actions of More which prove him to be a *man for all seasons*. You may want to discuss Whittinton's quotation or you may wish to discuss your own feelings about what it means to be "a man for all seasons."

5. Write an essay in which you fully explore the meaning of Sir Thomas More's statement to his daughter Meg during their last visit together in the Tower of London:

   > "Finally, it is not a matter of reason; finally, it is a matter of love."

6. Samuel Johnson, a famous English essayist, philosopher, writer, critic, said of Sir Thomas More:

   > "He was the person of the greatest virtue these islands [England] ever produced."

   Write a paper which effectively explains why this quote is true using your understanding and appreciation of this play.

7. " . . . when statesmen forsake their own private conscience for the sake of their public duties . . . they lead their country by a short route to chaos" (p. 13).

   Sir Thomas More was talking about people who forsake or ignore what is moral (in order to gain political security). Discuss three individuals who best illustrate this quotation. Use one from the play and two others you have researched who may be historical or fictional.

8. Discuss how two major characters misunderstood More and how each misunderstanding reveals a theme in the play.

9. Trace the imagery which runs throughout the play and explain the significance of it to major themes.

10. Discuss the characteristics of pragmatism and idealism as they function in the play.

11. Discuss how this play presents ideas that are relevant today.

12. The Common Man states, "I'm just a plain simple man and just want to keep out of trouble." Discuss to what extent his philosophy has permeated modern life. In what ways has it proven detrimental to both the individual and society?

13. Discuss various types of commitments made in this play.

14. Discuss what behavior is considered to be *human*. (You may wish to refer to More's discussion with Margaret in the Tower cell.) Then discuss how this behavior is important to the play.

Criticism Found in Magazines

America	106:452	January 6, '62
America	107:184–187	April 28, '62
Catholic World	194:255–256	January '62
Christian Century	79:317–318	December 15, '61
Journal of	21:116–117	Winter 86/87
Canadian Studies		
Life	52:55–57	January 12, '62
Macleans	99:51	August 18, '86
Nation	193:480	December 9, '61
New Republic	145:28–30	December 11, '61
New York	20:52–53	January 19, '87
New Yorker	37:117	December 2, '61
Newsweek	58:78	December 4, '61
Plays and Players	22:31+	April '75
Reporter	26:38	January 4, '61
Saturday Review	44:27	December 16, '61
Saturday Review	45:27	September 15, '62
Theatre Arts	46:10–11	February '62
Time	78:64	December 1, '61

Bibliography

Beckingsale, Bernard. *Thomas Cromwell, Tudor Minister*. Totowa, N.J.: Rowan and Little Field, 1978.

Bolt, Robert. *A Man for All Seasons*. New York, N.Y.: Vintage Books, 1962.

Ferguson, Charles W. *Naked to Mine Enemies*. Boston: Little Brown Co., 1958.

Gassner, John. *Dramatic Surroundings*. New York: Crown, 1968, pp. 508–510.

Gassner, John (ed.) *Reader's Encyclopedia of World Drama*. New York: Thomas Y. Cromwell, 1969, pp. 71–72.

A Man for all Seasons video/Zenger Video. 134 minutes, color. (Zenger Video, 10200 Jefferson Boulevard, P.O. Box 802, Culver City, CA 90232-0802, 1-800-421-4246)

"Modern Man for All Seasons," Esquire, December, 1962, p. 149.

Marius, Richard. *Thomas More: A Biography*. New York: Knopf, 1984.

Oberman, Heiko Augustinus. *Luther: Man between God and the Devil*. New Haven: Yale University Press, 1989.

Reynolds, Ernest. *Saint Sir Thomas More*. Milwaukee: Bruce Publishing Co., 1968.

Acknowledgments

For permission to reprint all works in this volume grateful acknowledgment is made to the following holders of copyright, publishers, or representatives.

Whole Book
Excerpts from *A Man for All Seasons* by Robert Bolt. Copyright © 1960, 1962 by Robert Bolt. Reprinted by permission of Random House, Inc., New York, New York.

Supplementary Materials
"Conscience and the Crown" by James H. Hansen. Copyright © 1979 by *Performing Arts Magazine*, Los Angeles, California. Reprinted by permission.

Novel/Drama Series

Novel

Across Five Aprils, Hunt
Adventures of Huckleberry Finn, Twain
Alice's Adventures in Wonderland/
    Through the Looking-Glass, Carroll
All Quiet on the Western Front, Remarque
All the King's Men, Warren
Animal Farm, Orwell/Book of the Dun Cow,
    Wangerin, Jr.
Anne Frank: The Diary of a Young Girl, Frank
The Autobiography of Miss Jane Pittman, Gaines
The Awakening, Chopin/Madame Bovary, Flaubert
Babbitt, Lewis
Beowulf/Grendel, Gardner
Billy Budd/Moby Dick, Melville
Brave New World, Huxley
The Bridge of San Luis Rey, Wilder
The Call of the Wild/White Fang, London
The Canterbury Tales, Chaucer
The Catcher in the Rye, Salinger
The Chosen, Potok
Cold Sassy Tree, Burns
Crime and Punishment, Dostoevsky
Cry, the Beloved Country, Paton
Dandelion Wine, Bradbury
A Day No Pigs Would Die, Peck
The Divine Comedy, Dante
Don Quixote, Cervantes
Dr. Zhivago, Pasternak
Fahrenheit 451, Bradbury
A Farewell to Arms, Hemingway
Frankenstein, Shelley
The Good Earth, Buck
The Grapes of Wrath, Steinbeck
Great Expectations, Dickens
The Great Gatsby, Fitzgerald
Gulliver's Travels, Swift
Hard Times, Dickens
The Heart Is a Lonely Hunter, McCullers
Heart of Darkness, Conrad
Hiroshima, Hersey/On the Beach, Shute
The Hound of the Baskervilles, Doyle
Incident at Hawk's Hill, Eckert/
    Where the Red Fern Grows, Rawls
Jane Eyre, Brontë
Johnny Tremain, Forbes
The Joy Luck Club, Tan
Julie of the Wolves, George/Island of the Blue Dolphins, O'Dell
The Jungle, Sinclair
The Killer Angels, Shaara
The Learning Tree, Parks
Les Miserables, Hugo
The Light in the Forest/A Country of Strangers, Richter
Little House in the Big Woods/Little House on the Prairie, Wilder
Lord of the Flies, Golding
Lord of the Rings, Tolkien
Mrs. Mike, Freedman/I Heard the Owl Call My Name, Craven
Murder on the Orient Express/
    And Then There Were None, Christie
My Antonia, Cather
The Natural, Malamud/Shoeless Joe, Kinsella
Night, Wiesel
Obasan, Kogawa
The Odyssey, Homer
The Old Man and the Sea, Hemingway/Ethan Frome, Wharton
The Once and Future King, White
The Pearl/Of Mice and Men, Steinbeck
Picture of Dorian Gray, Wilde/
    Dr. Jekyll and Mr. Hyde, Stevenson

The Pigman/Pigman's Legacy, Zindel
A Portrait of the Artist as a Young Man, Joyce
The Power and the Glory, Greene
Pride and Prejudice, Austen
Profiles in Courage, Kennedy
The Red Badge of Courage, Crane
The Return of the Native, Hardy
Roll of Thunder, Hear My Cry/Let the Circle Be Unbroken, Taylor
The Scarlet Letter, Hawthorne
A Separate Peace, Knowles
The Slave Dancer, Fox/I, Juan de Pareja, De Treviño
Song of Solomon, Morrison
The Sound and the Fury, Faulkner
Spoon River Anthology, Masters
The Stranger/The Plague, Camus
A Tale of Two Cities, Dickens
Tess of the D'Urbervilles, Hardy
To Kill a Mockingbird, Lee
To the Lighthouse, Woolf
Treasure Island, Stevenson
A Tree Grows in Brooklyn, Smith
Tuck Everlasting, Babbitt/Bridge to Terabithia, Paterson
Uncle Tom's Cabin, Stowe
Walkabout, Marshall
Watership Down, Adams
When the Legends Die, Borland
The Witch of Blackbird Pond, Speare/
    My Brother Sam Is Dead, Collier and Collier
A Wrinkle in Time, L'Engle/
    The Lion, the Witch and the Wardrobe, Lewis
Wuthering Heights, Brontë
The Yearling, Rawlings/The Red Pony, Steinbeck

Drama

Antigone, Sophocles
Arms and the Man/Saint Joan, Shaw
The Crucible, Miller
Cyrano de Bergerac, Rostand
Death of a Salesman, Miller
A Doll's House/Hedda Gabler, Ibsen
The Glass Menagerie, Williams
The Importance of Being Earnest, Wilde
Inherit the Wind, Lawrence and Lee
Long Day's Journey into Night, O'Neill
A Man for All Seasons, Bolt
The Miracle Worker, Gibson
The Night Thoreau Spent in Jail, Lawrence and Lee
Oedipus the King, Sophocles
Our Town, Wilder
The Playboy of the Western World/Riders to the Sea, Synge
Pygmalion, Shaw
A Raisin in the Sun, Hansberry
1776, Stone and Edwards
A Streetcar Named Desire, Williams
Tartuffe, Molière
Waiting for Godot, Beckett/
    Rosencrantz & Guildenstern Are Dead, Stoppard

Shakespeare

As You Like It
Hamlet
Henry V
Julius Caesar
King Lear
Macbeth
The Merchant of Venice

A Midsummer Night's Dream
Othello
Romeo and Juliet
The Taming of the Shrew
The Tempest
Twelfth Night

REV 10/93

THE PUBLISHER

All instructional materials identified by the TAP® (Teachers/Authors/Publishers) trademark are developed by a national network of teachers whose collective educational experience distinguishes the publishing objective of The Center for Learning, a non-profit educational corporation founded in 1970.

Concentrating on values-related disciplines, The Center publishes humanities and religion curriculum units for use in public and private schools and other educational settings. Approximately 300 language arts, social studies, novel/drama, life issues, and faith publications are available.

While acutely aware of the challenges and uncertain solutions to growing educational problems, The Center is committed to quality curriculum development and to the expansion of learning opportunities for all students. Publications are regularly evaluated and updated to meet the changing and diverse needs of teachers and students. Teachers may offer suggestions for development of new publications or revisions of existing titles by contacting

The Center for Learning

Administrative/Editorial Office
21590 Center Ridge Road
Rocky River, Ohio, 44116
(216) 331-1404 • FAX (216) 331-5414

For a free catalog, containing order and price information, and a descriptive listing of titles, contact

The Center for Learning

Shipping/Business Office
P.O. Box 910
Villa Maria, PA 16155
(412) 964-8083 • (800) 767-9090
FAX (412) 964-8992